A TUSCAN IN THE KITCHEN

RECIPES AND TALES FROM MY HOME

BY PINO LUONGO

WITH BARBARA RAIVES & ANGELA HEDERMAN

Clarkson N. Potter, Inc./Publishers
DISTRIBUTED BY CROWN PUBLISHERS, INC., NEW YORK

Photo credits: We would like to thank Jorgos Kap-
salis/ikon editions for permission to reproduce the
photographs on pages 2, 6, 7, 10 (bottom), 11, 14,
15, 37, 58, 88, 161, 205; Nicola Urbano for permission to reproduce the photographs on pages 10 (top
and middle), 36, 70, 188; Angela Hederman for permission to reproduce the photographs on pages 17,
19, 21, 27, 28, 30, 32, 35, 39, 53, 69, 89, 119, 129,
133, 161, 197, 217, 226; Alinari/Art Resource for
permission to reproduce the photographs on pages
4, 18, 23, 26, 56, 90, 91, 118, 128, 176, 204, 212,
216, 235; Snark/Art Resource for permission to
reproduce the picture on page 46; Scala/Art
Resource for permission to reproduce the paintings
on pages 68 and 196; SEF/Art Resource for permission to reproduce the photograph on page 177; and
Pino Luongo for permission to reproduce the photographs on pages 41, 178–179, and 206–207.

Our thanks to Carolyn Hart, Susan Bergholz,
Carol Southern, Gael Towey, Amy Schuler,
and the people of Tuscany.
All of you made this book possible.

C O N T E N T S

INTRODUCTION
8

VINO E CUCINA
EATING AND DRINKING IN TUSCANY
19

LA DISPENSA DI CUCINA
STOCKING A TUSCAN KITCHEN
27

LA CUCINA DEL BUON SENSO
THE ESSENCE OF TUSCAN COOKING
37

GLI ANTIPASTI
HUMBLE BEGINNINGS
41

I FUNGHI
THE JEWELS OF THE WOODS
57

ZUPPE E MINESTRE
THE SOUPS OF BREAD AND FANTASY
69

PASTA È BASTA
PASTA, THAT'S ALL
89

I RISOTTI

ROMANCING THE RISOTTO

119

IL PESCE

GRANDPA'S NETS AND GRANDMA'S POTS

129

LA CACCIAGIONE

HUNTING FOR GAME

161

LE CARNI

STEWED, ROASTED, AND GRILLED MEAT

177

IL POLLAME

BIRDS OF A FEATHER

197

I VEGETALI E LE INSALATE

VEGETABLES AND SALADS

205

I DOLCI

THE PERFECT ENDING

217

P. S. LAST NIGHT IN FLORENCE

234

INDEX

236

INTRODUCTION

My region is Tuscany. I was born in Tuscany and my family is basically Tuscan. My father came from the Neapolitan region, but that's another story. . . .

Tuscany is in the middle of Italy. It is shaped roughly like a triangle, with the Tyrrhenian Sea on one side and the Appennini Mountains on the other. On one side of the triangle, the smooth, soft hills of Siena and Arezzo slope toward the *piano*, which are the flatlands of Maremma. Within this triangle, there are nine beautiful cities.

At one time Tuscany was a totally wild region that for two thousand years—from the Etruscans to the Tuscans—was treated with such love and care that it became a paradise. The small rural communities as much as the big cities have set the rhythm of Tuscan life.

Even as Tuscany looks to the future, it holds on to whatever is good from the past. We feel as if we belong to a special part of the world where each generation is connected to all the ones that went before in a continuous, harmonious line.

The distinctive Tuscan character was formed by traditions, and the essence of the land has not been changed by invaders, natural disasters, or outside influences. Tuscans have their own language, their own ways of suffering, their own ways of believing, which have produced a body of literature and art that is among the greatest in Europe. Giotto was a Tuscan, as were Donatello, Leonardo da Vinci, Michelangelo, and of course Dante.

Probably whatever I say about Tuscany can't be proved or documented. How can I transfer to paper the way I feel when I see a certain Tuscan landscape? How can I tell about what I hear and smell when I go back home? There are no explanations. Tuscany is part of me; it's the place where I belong.

My relationship with the food of Tuscany is very simple: it was the food of my childhood. I grew up loving the countryside of Tuscan cuisine and the way people used the land. Tuscany is a region of peasants who have always worked the land, growing their own vegetables, keeping their own animals. They have never been a rich people, but they have always found inventive ways to cook something wonderful with the things they had.

We say that if you grow up, as I did, in a family in which every resource has to be used 100 percent, you become an imaginative cook so that, one day, if your life improves —even if you can afford to buy expensive things—you still have the ability to create something special from the few ingredients you have.

Tuscan cuisine gives you this chance. It encourages you to adapt and improve on the original, because Tuscan food has never become an institution. It has always been open to the personal efforts and imagination that make better-tasting dishes. In Tuscany we don't want chefs cooking for us—we want Mamma! If all the mammas of Tuscany were instructed to cook a certain dish, no two would come out the same. Tuscans use only natural products, with all their peculiarities, so it's impossible for everything to be cooked the same way.

And Tuscans don't believe it should be. Our regional cookbook has a cover and a first page, but the last page hasn't been written yet. We keep at it, and we're still open to many different experiences.

Most cookbooks give exact amounts of this and that, but I never learned about timing and quantities —I did everything by instinct. If you make a mistake in tablespoons, it's not going to hurt you. You don't need a prescription for cooking food; you're the person in charge. Don't be afraid to follow your feelings. Be flexible, be creative—abandon your inhibitions and have fun. When it looks good and feels right, you'll know it. Trust yourself —you know better than to stuff anchovies into a profiterole. One day you'll have the pleasure of making something so good you'll know it's a triumph that came from your imagination and not some rule or formula. As in love, there are no rules for cooking. Everything should be done with feeling.

In Tuscany the kitchen is the center of the home, and food is a big part of the important events in life. Cooking shouldn't be an ordeal. It should be the pleasure of creating something you want to share with the people you care most about. You don't have to feel impotent when you open the refrigerator and all you see are tomatoes, some butter, eggs, maybe some leftover green beans, and a piece of cheese. Sauté the beans in some good olive oil, put in the eggs with some salt and pepper, sprinkle the whole thing with a bit of cheese, and you'll have what we call a frittata. Serve this with fresh country bread and chilled sliced tomatoes, and sit down with a friend and a bottle of wine. If you keep the meal simple and spontaneous, it leaves room for more complicated experiences.

For me, cooking is about creating magic from something very real. My experience as an actor led me to become a cook. Acting is an ephemeral art—it vanishes like smoke. But cooking is very real and lets me create something of substance from my imagination and emotions.

We have a saying in Italy that good love starts in your stomach. You never see anyone go through the best day of his or her life on an empty stomach. Speaking for all Tuscans, I know that good food is essential to day-to-day life. A bad meal certainly won't put you in a better mood, but a great meal can be an event you'll remember forever.

PINO LUONGO

Our first encounter with Pino Luongo took place in the middle of a snowstorm that had paralyzed New York City and prevented us from going to our favorite restaurant. Instead, we got no farther than the newly opened restaurant next door to our loft in Greenwich Village. Midway through the pasta course we knew we had stumbled on culinary genius.

While we lingered over the espresso, the lights were dimmed and the half-deserted restaurant was filled with the sound of Mahler's Fourth Symphony. For a moment nothing moved but the swirling snow that was illuminated by the lights above the high glass doors in front of the restaurant. The effect was magical, and we knew that something more than food was being offered here.

There followed many meals and conversations with Pino at Il Cantinori. When springtime came, the glass doors were folded back, letting in the street sounds of the Village, and diners lingered on the terra-cotta terrace. We would sit with Pino sipping a Campari at the bar, and he would describe the people and food of Tuscany. His thoughts on the subject of food often ranged as far as religion, death, and sex, about which he spoke in a distinctly Tuscan voice—the lyrical pairing of the aristocrat and the peasant. The setting was the Tuscan countryside: its hill towns, vineyards, and fishing ports. Among the cast of characters was an eccentric grandmother who hung eels on a clothesline to dry; a beautiful country girl from the tiny village of Femmina Morta, who showed Pino how to eat soup without a spoon; the bandits of Maremma, who smoked cigars with the lit ends in their mouths.

Pino told us about the history and regional customs of Tuscany, about family gatherings, and about personal adventures that make up the background of his culinary experience. As he shared his irrepressible enthusiasm for food and life, it occurred to us that this simple and ancient country cuisine fit into new ways of cooking and eating in America and should be expressed in a book about the food of Tuscany—something combining Pino's recipes and stories, his robust and unrestrained ideas about food, and their translation into the American kitchen.

We had a strong feeling that his type of food could be cooked easily at home. We had never felt that way about the food in French restaurants because it always seemed too complicated to try, too clouded and sauced over with mystery. But in this peasant style, the rules were freer, compared to the formalized traditions in which the cook had to be precise and skilled in order to succeed. The Tuscan approach to cooking seemed joyous and free of the rigid rules that make food an institution in some countries.

From this we should have foreseen that Pino's idea of a recipe and ours were entirely different, but it still came as a shock when he would not tell us ingredient amounts or cooking times. When we asked how long to cook something, he said, "Why do you think God created forks?" Clearly, he meant that the only way to tell when something was done was to stab it with a fork, and if it was tender, it was done.

If we cooked a sauce down too much, Pino told us to add some liquid. We asked, "Broth? Wine? Water?" and he said, "How can I answer that? What do you want to taste more of? It's a free country."

His responses were infuriating at first, but they made perfect sense. We realized we were so locked into conventional cookbook formulas that we had never developed spontaneity in the kitchen. It was no wonder that when we invited people to dinner, we spent days devising the menu, then were nervous wrecks trying to orchestrate time with the guests and still make sure the food "turned out."

Then one day in the middle of an editing session we found ourselves hungry for lunch, reluctant to go out to eat, and faced with a refrigerator of odds and ends: some tomatoes, part of an eggplant, a red onion. We threw them together into a sauce. We could hardly believe how good it was. We didn't have a recipe; we didn't have amounts or times. But Pino hadn't set us adrift without a map. He had taught us the basic, simple techniques of a Tuscan sauce. And it worked! The techniques were never too complicated, never too involved, never too delicate. We found that most of the work in a good Tuscan dish comes from stretching the imagination and developing a personal way of combining a small number of ingredients. We even stopped thinking about recipes and started thinking about combinations of ingredients.

All of a sudden, we felt free to experiment and find our own way in the kitchen. If we ran out of one of the suggested ingredients for a sauce, so what? We added more of something else. If we varied the amount of prosciutto in a dish, it never made the dish bad—just different. With Pino as our guide, cooking became an exhilarating experience. We had come around to Pino's way of thinking.

This was the beginning of the liberation process. We found that if we followed some simple techniques, the food always "turned out"—and often more to our taste than when we followed someone else's formula. We were no longer inhibited and felt free to double amounts or leave something out completely. The same combinations were frequently a little different, but always good. The chief characteristic of Tuscan cuisine that allows such leeway in the kitchen is its basic simplicity and common sense.

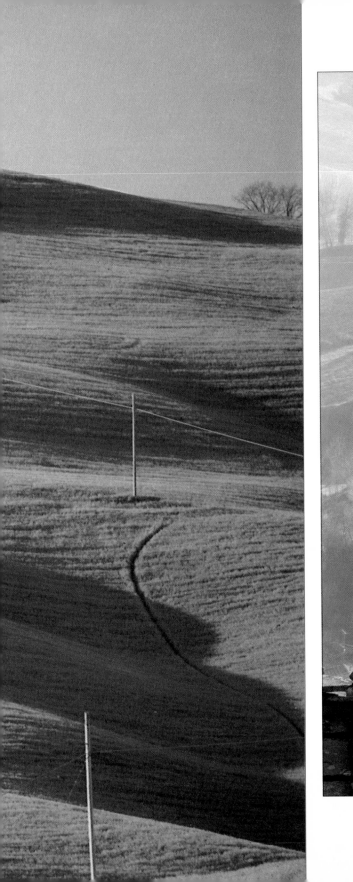

One of the other happy discoveries along the way was that we were using a basic set of ingredients over and over again. The success of Tuscan cooking doesn't depend on number. If you stock your pantry in a modest but practical way, you will simplify your life immeasurably. With these ingredients on hand, you can make any of the dishes in this book with the addition of only a handful of fresh ingredients—usually no more than three, which are few enough so you can go through the express line at the market.

We were surprised, even shocked, to discover that we never became bored with the tastes. We found the variety to be astonishing, because we were adding and subtracting elements according to our tastes and our moods. One day, a pasta sauce would be laden with sausage, and on the next day it became essentially a tomato sauce.

A handful of truly memorable ingredients, which are used sparingly but consistently throughout Tuscan cooking, sustains its vitality and freshness—things like pecorino cheese, balsamic vinegar, imported plum tomatoes, and the best virgin olive oil.

For example, grilled trout that has been marinated in olive oil and balsamic vinegar is a combination we had never heard of before. We could never have imagined its sophistication. But the first bite made it clear that this is truly the cuisine that sprang from the cradle of the Renaissance and is heir to its unequaled brilliance and regard for style. It is impossible to imagine that Renaissance men and women left behind their interest in art when they stepped into the kitchen. Indeed they did not, and this inspiration still animates Tuscan food today.

While other Italians may refer to Tuscans as "bean-eaters," who but an aristocratic Florentine would take that as a compliment as he offered you a plate of the first raw fava beans of spring, tossed with crumbled pecorino and glistening with newly pressed olive oil. With great pride, and only three ingredients, he has elevated the lowly bean to a triumph. Again and again, this cooking reaffirms the truth that simplicity is elegance in its purest form.

You will find that when you simplify your shopping and relax your attitude toward cooking, you will cook with more spontaneity and joy. Yet these are dishes special enough for company. When people come over to have a drink, you can invite them, on the spur of the moment, to stay for dinner. Don't order out for a pizza. And don't panic. You have everything you need in your pantry and a hundred ways to combine them in Pino's recipes. It's not an accident that the best cooking in Tuscany is found at home. It's the place where Tuscans' passionate love for food meets their passionate love for family and friends.

BARBARA RAIVES
ANGELA HEDERMAN

VINO E CUCINA

EATING
AND
DRINKING
IN
TUSCANY

There is a special breakfast I look forward to when I arrive in Rome after the night flight from New York. On the drive home to Tuscany I make a detour to the tiny village of Talamone, where there is a place called—can you believe it?—Fonteblanda Morgan. The place is so small that the owner first has to twist his pants to turn around. The original owner was called Morgan because in Italy that's what we call anyone with only one eye, after the pirate with the black eye patch.

This Morgan would make you a breakfast of tiny white pizzas, which are very, very good. Before baking the dough, he sprinkled it with salt and olive oil. While the pizzas were still hot, he spread them with ricotta cheese and added three or four anchovies. You just fold them over and eat them in one bite. Unfortunately, Morgan is not there anymore, but his spirit can still be found in many small restaurants and trattorias in Tuscany. These are the places I search out because they offer the flavors and tastes that nourish me when I'm away.

So I would suggest to someone who is not familiar with Tuscany that he or she get a detailed map and then not worry about where to eat. Just go by intuition. Don't look for a fancy place to eat, because that will give you the wrong idea about Tuscan food. Instead, go to a fam-ily-run trattoria where you see the local people eating and order from the simple, small menu that they have every day. If you eat this way, it's hard to have a bad meal in Tuscany.

Tuscans believe that the best food you can eat is in your own home. This is the only thing to keep in mind when you are eating out because the inspiration for a good Tuscan restaurant is home cooking. You can find many good restaurants in Tuscany, but I have chosen to mention the following, because, like the recipes in this book, they reflect a philosophy rooted in the many regional tastes and flavors of the Tuscan cuisine.

When I'm in Grosseto, I always stop at the restaurant of my friend Giancarlo. Giancarlo has an intel-lectual approach to the kitchen. He has great knowledge of the history and traditions of his region, and he offers authentic dishes to the patrons who come to his restaurant. These are the same dishes that were good when the region was very poor and survival was all that mattered— dishes like Aquacotta (page 72), Zuppa Maremmana (page 78), and Pasta e Fagioli (page 83). These dishes tell you that even when Tus-cans were very poor, they still knew how to eat. When you go to Gian-carlo's restaurant, you know you are not only going to eat something

Page 18: **Chianti fair**

good, but you will learn something as well. For him, running a restaurant is not just a job, it's a mission, giving Giancarlo the opportunity to preserve a part of the past that is still important to the present.

Giancarlo uses only local produce, wines, and oils from the region. He describes the taste and bouquet of his wines in an elegant and poetic way, and he displays the largest selection of olive oil that I have ever seen anywhere. He presents the oils on a cart to the interested customer, and he has analyzed the acidic property and different taste of each one. He's a pure intellectual.

Driving from the flatlands of Grosseto uphill toward Montalcino, you start to have the first scent of this region of Tuscany. But no matter how you approach

it, when you see the smooth, soft hills dotted with pines, cypress trees, and old oaks, you will be in a unique part of Tuscany. It seems that everything was planted to please the eye and all the farms and houses were placed not with indifference but to blend in perfect harmony with the landscape. This landscape is one of the most inspirational works created by the Tuscans.

Montalcino is also known for producing some of the most pleasant, well-balanced, and highly esteemed wines in the world. Stroll along the old main street, look at the medieval buildings, and stop in at the local wine shop. When it is time for lunch or dinner, go to Edgardo's place. It is very different from Giancarlo's. Whereas Giancarlo is extremely earthy and takes pride in serving authentic regional dishes, Edgardo is a Florentine

Olive oil tasting

artist who is reinterpreting, with imagination, six hundred years of Tuscan gastronomy—a little bit fancy, a little bit frivolous, but he knows his food and its background. He just feels that in order to please he has to adapt to the modern way of eating, although he always has a reason for the way he puts dishes together. Even when Edgardo serves squash blossoms stuffed with parsley mayonnaise, he does it because the sharp lemony taste helps you appreciate even more the traditional Pasticcio, a sweet pepper stew (see page 51), that follows.

Giancarlo and Edgardo are characteristic of many people I know in Tuscany because they are so opinionated; one stands for one point of view and the other for the extreme opposite—but both are pure Tuscan.

Going north from Montalcino, you will find yourself on the swinging, winding, up-and-down road to Siena. I think Siena is the most breathtakingly beautiful city in the world. As you approach it, the earth-colored buildings appear suddenly like a dark and brooding silhouette against the sky. Siena is not like any other town in Tuscany. It is a bloody soldier-type of town, built with the ferocity and strength that have endured many wars. It is a very moody place, and you can still feel the darkness of its history today.

If you want to get a sense of the Sienese cuisine, let yourself venture through the tiny streets that always end up in the Piazza del Campo. It isn't difficult here to find a family-run trattoria that offers the local specialties such as game, red meat dishes, and soup—especially the bread soups for which Siena is famous.

North from Siena, as you get closer to Florence, you come into the essence of Tuscany. Since the time of the Medicis, Florentines have managed to appropriate and adapt for their own kitchens all the best from the Tuscan countryside. It may seem unusual to go to Florence and ignore the fancy city restaurants— which are legitimate—but I prefer the gutsy dishes that are characteristic of Tuscany, even when I'm in the cities. So my culinary tour takes us to two of my favorite restaurants: Sostanza and Coco Lezzone.

As you enter Sostanza, you see two huge flasks of wine on the white-tile bar (one for white wine and one for red), a large glass jar of Pratesi cookies, and another of Vin Santo, the holy wine to dip them in for dessert. This gives you the tone of the place right away. Beyond the bar, in the dining room, are two long dining tables with an open kitchen facing out so you can see what's cooking. This is a simple trattoria, yes, but what they are doing with food here is what you would find in a Tuscan home.

Sostanza offers its own ribollita,

incredible artichokes baked in individual crocks, a variety of lamb dishes, and its own beefsteak Florentine style. The menu is limited and not always printed; sometimes the proprietor just tells you what he has prepared that day. But whatever he is serving, you can expect the best to eat in Florence, even though the environment may be as simple as home.

Coco Lezzone has the same feeling as Sostanza, the same wine, and the same cookies on the bar. The menu the day you are there may be a frittata with onions, pasta with zucchini, rabbit stew in white wine, and an artichoke salad. But whatever you order, the meal is sure to end with Pratesi and Vin Santo.

From Florence, the road west to the coast leads you through Lucca. The old city is surrounded by ramparts in a region of dark, wooded hills and rich soil. The roughness

and strength of the land and its people seem more closely connected to Maremma and the south of Tuscany than to the adjoining inland regions.

I like to stop just outside of Lucca in an old mill that is now a trattoria called Il Vipore. It is run by a family who serves a few unusual northern Tuscan dishes made with farro. Farro is a dark wheat that can be made into antipasti or used in soups and stews. But if you want some of the best seafood in the Mediterranean, save your appetite for Pisa or Livorno.

Pisa is a beautiful town with the most incredible tower in the world. There is a market in the old part of Pisa that is surrounded by little trattorias serving the freshest seafood, exquisitely prepared. You will want to concentrate on local dishes such as Cacciucco (page 151), or a special squid stew with peas (page

Two men, a horse, and 3,000 liters of Chianti

152). The local specialties here are made with a variety of shellfish, fish, or squid and seasonal vegetables. Only in Pisa or Livorno will you have an opportunity to appreciate these particular dishes, so be sure to try a few. But remember, as elsewhere in Tuscany, look out for the small, family-run trattorias, even in the cities and towns.

I have to be honest: Edgardo is fine, I like Giancarlo, Sostanza, and Coco Lezzone, but I can never, never—even if the meal is not at the same level—replace in my affections any of the tiny, very simple, familial places that have the tables outside overlooking the vineyards and near the olive trees—those local spots that offer a simple menu, sometimes not even a menu, but just what they are serving that day.

If you are driving around the countryside and you see a sign—Da Maria—you will know it's Maria's place. It's not a sophisticated restaurant; the name is personal and it lets you know Maria doesn't care to have the attention. "I'm Maria," she's telling you, "I'm here. I'm cooking my own cuisine. Come over. I'm growing vegetables and raising animals in my backyard, and that's what you'll eat."

So if you happen to be lost in the countryside, look for the best setting, like the place up in the hills with the tables underneath vineyard roofings. You can't go there and request something sophisticated and elaborate, but you don't mind because you'll get atmosphere and fresh air instead. These places are really the soul of Tuscan gastronomy.

Bagnoli is a restaurant hidden in the hills in the middle of nowhere. You realize that not everything on the menu is going to be available, and probably nothing has changed over the years. The attitude of the patrons and Signora Claudia, the proprietor, is that they like things the way they are. She doesn't think about how to please people coming from the city who have a different idea about food. Probably, if you were sitting in Florence and were served slightly stale bread, you would say, "Waiter, this bread is stale." Up here, you don't complain. For some reason, you forgive everything—maybe because it's genuine. The wine is made locally; it's probably not perfect, not full of harmony, not well balanced—but who cares? The cuisine is not first class; it's a very rustic peasant cuisine—uncontaminated; the way it used to be and the way it still is.

A good restaurant should have a very strong personal feeling, and it's not all about food. Broiled chicken served in a million-dollar city restaurant will never taste as great to me as the grilled chicken in Bagnoli, up in the mountains.

Tuscans like wine as much as they do food, so in every town and city in Tuscany, there is a vineria—a local or neighborhood place where people meet, but instead of offering food, they have wine. You can buy a bottle to take home or have a glass right on the premises. When I was a kid I used to go with my grandfather in the morning to his favorite vineria, where he would have what is called a cicchettino—a small shot of wine guaranteed to make you feel good all day. From Florence to Orbetello, up in the mountains and down to the sea, this has been a tradition among Tuscan men for generations, and to some extent it still is today.

Everyone in Tuscany wants his own plot of ground to grow grapes so that he can make his own wine. In a Tuscan home, no one will try to impress you with a vintage estate-bottled wine or a fine Brunello or Chianti. Instead, the best you can be offered is a wine that is made at home or at least locally.

My father didn't own his own little vineyard, but he had his own contadino who lived in the hills above Florence and sold wine by the liter from his house. My father would buy a hundred liters of white wine and a hundred liters of red at one time. This was only enough for my family for a short time; with all the friends and relatives coming in and out of the house, it usually didn't last long.

My father is not a Tuscan. He's one of the mistakes of the family; he's from the South. And I have to be honest. He doesn't have very good taste in wine. He drinks red wine chilled, and he almost taught my mother to drink it the same way. When I was old enough to be aware, I put a stop to that.

I don't believe that red wine only goes with certain dishes and white wine with others. It's the body and the bouquet of the wine that are important. I don't have any problem drinking a young red wine with Cacciucco, a fish stew with a strong taste of garlic and tomatoes; and in the summer I like a white wine with Ossobuco (page 185).

I remember as a young boy I often had to endure an upset stomach because the wine offered at home was so rich and thick you had to eat it with a spoon. The juice had been pressed from the grapes by people with bare feet, put into barrels, and then into large flasks. It was never carried to the final step of straining the skin and pulp. The wine we drink today is not the same thick, rich wine that people used to drink a long time ago. My grandfather used to say, "Today we drink the wine, but once we used to eat the wine."

LA DISPENSA DI CUCINA

STOCKING

A

TUSCAN

KITCHEN

When you stock a Tuscan kitchen you need to have a certain vision more than you need advice. To the shoppers who crowd the supermarket with lists two feet long and shopping carts full of produce, then walk out followed by supermarket kids carrying lots of bags, and who, once home, start to worry about how and where to store everything, I suggest this: think about a very tiny Tuscan lady who, in her kitchen, has stored enough pasta, olive oil, dried beans, canned tomatoes, garlic, and so on to be ready for any event.

With not too much strength in her arms, she has carried a very small plastic or leather shopping bag and gone out for a walk to see what's available at the local market. "Oh, it's Thursday. I'm going to stop at the fish market because they have fresh fish today." And then she picks a few anchovies to make anchovies with garlic, parsley, olive oil, and white wine. Next, she asks the butcher, "You have a new pig today, yes? Give me four chops. I'm coming back in five minutes." She goes to the poultry shop and gets four or five eggs. Then she goes to the vegetable market. "It's May. You have any good cherries?" "Sure, I've got cherries." She also picks up rugola (arugula), cucumbers, tomatoes. On the way home, she buys a loaf of bread at the bakery. And she heads toward home, content in the knowledge that she has had her daily walk and completed her duties as a housewife.

So keep this vision in mind, even if you don't live in a small hill town in Tuscany, and stock your kitchen with the following list of ingredients.

To make life easier, I've divided the ingredients by the place they're kept in any Tuscan kitchen. Items that can be stored without refrigeration because they are not perishable or they are dried are listed under Pantry (La Dispensa). Ingredients that require refrigeration are listed under Cold Storage (La Cantina). At this point, if you have a pantry and a refrigerator well-stocked with those items used repeatedly in these recipes, all you need to do is to buy these few fresh items that the recipes list under Market (Il Mercato).

Olive oil at rest in urns

Preceding pages: **Market in Tuscany, 1887 and 1987**

PANTRY	COLD STORAGE
Olive oil	Garlic
Corn oil	Red onions
Imported canned plum tomatoes	Fresh parsley
Tomato paste	Celery
Wine—red, white, vermouth	Carrots
Vinegar—red wine, white wine, balsamic	Potatoes
Pasta—penne, tubettini, farfalle, rotelle, rigatoni, spaghetti	Parmesan cheese
Italian Arborio rice (or long-grain Italian rice)	Lemons
Yellow cornmeal	Unsalted butter
Flour—all-purpose, pastry	Eggs
Sugar	Milk
Bread crumbs	Broth—chicken, beef, fish, vegetable
Beans—chick-peas, lentils, cannellini, black beans, red beans, lima beans	
Dried porcini	
Olives—black and green, Gaeta or Niçoise	
Juniper berries	
Anchovies	
Capers	
Assorted herbs (dried if fresh are unavailable)	
Coriander—seeds and ground	
Nutmeg	
Cinnamon	
Crushed red pepper	
Black pepper	
Salt	
Cayenne	
Raisins	
Almonds	
Walnuts	
Pignolis	
Vin Santo (Italian dessert wine)	

Enough about lists and classifications. Let's talk about some of the most important elements of Tuscan cooking.

OLIVE OIL

The classification of "extra virgin" is the most important consideration when you're shopping for olive oil. It's a guarantee that the olives were hand picked from the trees and the oil has been pressed in the old system, with stone wheels and without the use of heat. Also, look on the label to see if the olives were grown and the oil produced and bottled on the same estate. This assures you of extreme quality control. These oils are expensive, but worth it. Among the best are olive oils that come from Tuscany, Liguria, and Umbria.

I do not like olive oil that has had an aromatic essence of sage or thyme added. It's like putting Chanel perfume on a baby's bottom. Kids smell good by themselves, so why put perfume on top? You don't need it.

When you're sautéeing or frying, you can substitute corn oil for olive oil. It's more economical, and a good-quality corn oil can safely replace olive oil in the first stages of cooking. Olive oil can be used for cooking, of course, but its main purpose is to flavor, so it's best left the way it is—raw, natural. Olive oil can always be added to top off a soup or stew: it's like a heavenly coat.

You can add olive oil to stop salt if you put too much in a dish, but only if the amount wasn't too great. If the dish is much too salty, it's best just to throw it out.

Fresh-squeezed olive oil , when it is totally unfiltered and nothing has been added, is the best natural medicine in the world. It makes the intestines function better; it's also good for the liver and the pancreas. When you know you're going to drink a lot, just take a spoonful of olive oil and you won't have a hangover.

ODORI

The foundation of many Tuscan dishes, such as soups, sauces, and stews, is odori—a mixture of finely chopped red onions, celery, carrots, parsley, and sometimes garlic in any combination you want.

To make odori, first dampen the bottom of a pan with olive oil and then lightly cover it with the chopped vegetables. When you look inside the pan, you'll see a beautiful, colorful combination of orange carrots, light green celery, dark green parsley, and red onions. Sauté the vegetables over medium heat until they turn blond from cooking and the oil has been absorbed. Then continue with the necessary steps to complete whatever soup, stew, or sauce you're planning to make.

GARLIC

Garlic is something you always want to eat, but you never want to smell like. The power of garlic excels in certain dishes like Spaghetti con Aglio, Olio, e Peperoncino (page 111) or Fettunta (page 43), but in most other dishes, once the garlic has been browned, get rid of it, especially if you are preparing something delicate. The garlic flavor should be there, but not there.

There's a saying we have in Italy: *Vorrei ma non posso* —"I would like to but I can't." You have to feel that way about garlic. Tasting it is like flirting when you were a kid—you want more but you can't get it.

A Note About Garlic:
In most recipes in which garlic is used, it is first smashed with the heel of your hand or the flat side of a large knife.

HERBS

I would like to say once and for all that you don't need to limit certain herbs to certain dishes. Instead,

I suggest that you get familiar with different herbs, their tastes, their effects on certain dishes, the way they react in sauces, and then you won't have to limit yourself to rosemary with fish, or sage with game, or bay leaves with red meat. I make all kinds of dishes with all kinds of herbs.

My favorite common herbs are sage, basil, rosemary, tarragon, thyme, and bay leaves. Among the less common ones are fresh mint leaves, nepitella, catmint (catnip). I don't follow any rules when I use herbs; I just use the knowledge that I gained through trial and error, experimenting with how different tastes work together.

To become familiar with all the herbs, especially the ones mentioned, get to know them, experiment with them, and don't be afraid to use them in different dishes. There are so many ways of changing the taste of different kinds of dishes, whether appetizers, pasta sauces, main courses, or even slices of bread. Nothing here is standardized; it's a total improvisation based on an acquired knowledge of how these ingredients taste separately and an imagining of how they will taste together. Knowing the herbs, having this deep knowledge, allows you to generate so many varieties of dishes with just a few ingredients.

For a long time I thought I could use bay leaves only with certain foods. Then I found out this is not true. I put bay leaves with any kind of game—one of my favorite dishes is sweetbreads in browned butter with bay leaves and sage. Bay leaves and sage can even substitute for each other. I have started to make pasta sauces and ravioli with bay leaves. For ravioli, I just sauté the dried leaves with smoked duck breast. It's truly excellent.

With game, I also love to use rosemary and tarragon together; it's a very audacious combination. I love rosemary with sage and basil with mint. Basil and mint are especially good with spinach, so my Risotto con Spinaci (page 122) always has these two herbs. Parsley goes everywhere; it's a complementary kind of herb. It doesn't have originality on its own, except in a dish that I remember Giancarlo Bini cooked for me the first time I went to his restaurant in Grosseto. It was spaghetti with garlic, a little butter, Parmesan cheese, and lots of parsley. In that dish, you could appreciate the parsley by itself.

The peasant in Tuscany has always had a secret way of using herbs, and those herbs can change a dish dramatically. No matter what, even if the family were starving to death and a dish were made from the poorest ingredients, the peasant always added the final touch—the particular taste of aromatic herbs. And people say peasants are ignorant? I think they show great knowledge of their environment and the land they work.

Normally, I say to stay away from any vegetables grown in a greenhouse. Maybe I sound a little bit like the man who wants the wife drunk and a full bottle of wine. He wants everything. But I would like to make an exception to that rule where herbs are concerned. In the last three years I've been buying fresh herbs all year long, and that means that in certain seasons they must come from greenhouses. They are exceptionally good nonetheless. In markets all over the country fresh herbs are now available throughout the year.

If you want, you can grow herbs yourself in pots on a sunny windowsill in winter, or outside on a terrace in summer.

Although some herbs are good dried—bay leaves and oregano, for instance—sage and rosemary are much better fresh. And with thyme, there is a big difference between fresh and dried.

In my restaurant I keep herbs in quantity. I always buy pounds of everything. But even if you buy fresh herbs and dry them yourself, they are still useful.

Unless they are grown in a greenhouse, not all herbs are available during the winter, so it's smart to grow or buy fresh herbs in season to keep in your pantry for the winter. If you dry sage, oregano, rosemary, tarragon, thyme, and bay leaves at home they will turn out 100 percent better than if you buy them dried at the supermarket.

Some Notes About My Favorite Herbs:
BASIL Basil goes well with just about everything, whether you use it fresh and raw or cooked in a sauce. It is not pungent tasting, although it is aromatic. Always use fresh basil.

BAY LEAVES Bay leaves are extremely fragrant and have a sour bite that goes well with the sweet taste of kidneys, sweetbreads, and livers.

MINT Mint is delicious added to salads, sauces, and game, but always add it at the end of the cooking process. Only use it fresh.

OREGANO This herb grows wild at high altitudes. It was known for its medicinal properties, but now it's used mostly in the kitchen. It is excellent with potatoes, rice, tomatoes, and roasts.

ROSEMARY Among the aromatic herbs used in Tuscany,

rosemary is one of the most well known, most used, and many people think the best tasting. Sprigs of rosemary are often used as a basting brush. Dip a full branch in olive oil and brush it on whatever you're grilling.

SAGE Sage is excellent with roasted meat, but also good with stew, game, and even fish. Always use it fresh—and add it at the end of the cooking process.

THYME This herb makes a good addition to sauces. Add it at the end of the cooking process, or you'll lose the aroma. Always use it fresh.

TOMATOES

Maybe men are for all seasons, but not tomatoes. You can never expect to have a good, sparkling tomato taste from "man-made" tomatoes grown in a greenhouse. I use fresh salad (beefsteak) or plum tomatoes in salads only when they're in season, and I only use fresh plum tomatoes for sauces and stews when they are *very* ripe.

The tomato is a generous, unfancy product that Mother Nature allows to flourish in the Mediterranean area in large quantities. If they are picked early in the season when they are still slightly orange in color and not too juicy, they are excellent in salads. Later, when they are very ripe, I make them into a Filetto di

Pomodoro (page 105), which I use in certain dishes such as fresh pasta or the tiny tagliolini. When the tomato is so fresh, so tasty, and so ripe, you want to cook it as little as possible.

If you're making a stewed dish like an ossobuco, which you cook for a long time, leave the skins on the tomatoes because actually they add extra taste and texture to the dish.

As soon as the season is over, it's not a bad idea to consider using just the good-quality imported canned tomatoes. Even in Italy we don't have tomatoes all year long. In the winter we used canned tomatoes because they are put in cans when they are ripe, with their own natural juice. They are excellent. When you use canned tomatoes, squeeze them in your hand until the lumps and juice are no longer separate. Be careful to take out the hard yellow stem ends if there are any—they're the only part that is not very good.

PASTA

I suggest you buy imported dry pastas, since they are easier to cook al dente than the domestic varieties. It's important to start checking for doneness after about three or four minutes. When you bite into pasta, your teeth will tell you if it's done. Spinach and whole wheat pastas are good too and can be used in any recipe. But remember—the cooking times will vary.

Among the fresh pastas, the most commonly used in Tuscany are tagliatelle—a flat, thin noodle—and tagliolini, which is even thinner. Fresh pasta is as important in Tuscan cooking as dry pasta because it is good with gamy and complicated sauces. Dry pastas—such as spaghetti, penne, rigatoni, and all the other commercial shapes—even though they originally came from southern Italy, are used all over Italy. They are best with the least elaborate sauces and are especially appreciated with seafood sauces.

ARBORIO RICE

Rice is divided into two categories: soft, which is an opaque grain, and hard, which is a bright, white transparent grain. Arborio is a particular kind of hard-grain rice that is cultivated in the north of Italy. No self-respecting Tuscan would use anything but Arborio rice in a risotto, because it guarantees that each grain will be separate after it is cooked, and that's what distinguishes the dish.

Arborio rice is available in Italian markets and selected supermarkets throughout the country.

BREAD

Whether Tuscan bread is made with whole wheat or white flour, it is unsalted because centuries ago Tuscany was such a poor country that many people couldn't afford to pay the tax levied on salt. Necessity became a tradition when it was found that the absence of salt enhanced without altering the flavor of food served with this bread.

A Note About Bread:
Any time bread is mentioned in this book, I mean a loaf of crusty peasant bread.

BEANS

The urge to eat beans is so innate in the Tuscan people that they are used in every season, whether fresh or dried, in salads, soups, stews, or with roasts. In Tuscan cooking the most frequently used dried beans are cannellini beans, red beans, lentils, chick-peas, and lima beans. The fresh beans we like are red-eyed beans, fava beans, and all the shell beans that are fresh in summer.

HOT RED PEPPERS

Fresh or dried, a hot pepper is the spiciest vegetable in nature, and it helps give sparkle and pungency to any dish. In the south of Italy, fresh hot red pepper is considered a source of energy if eaten between two slices of bread and with dreams of a better life in your head.

PIGNOLIS

In Tuscany, there are miles and miles of coastline edged with pine woods that yield pignolis. Their abundance in Tuscany makes pignolis less expensive than in the United States but still extremely appreciated. We mostly use them in desserts, some game dishes, and sauces such as pesto.

VINEGAR

The vinegars I use most are red or white wine vinegar because of the particular taste they bring to a dish. I find that vinegar is always complementary if used sparingly. I also like the balsamic vinegars that are available now. They are as fragrant as cologne, but, just as with cologne, be careful not to overdo it.

Tuscan country deli

LA CUCINA DEL BUON SENSO

THE

ESSENCE

OF

TUSCAN

COOKING

Ingredients are the essence of Tuscan cooking. In the same way that you put together letters to make a word, you put together ingredients to make a dish. My attitude about food begins with shopping. The way a dish turns out depends much more on the ingredients you buy than on your cooking technique. Once you get the freshest ingredients, most of the important work has been done. In Tuscany, the farmer, the fisherman, and the hunter have more power over the table than the chef.

Many people tend to decide ahead what they want for dinner, make a list of the ingredients they need, and then go out and buy them. But what if the eggplants aren't very good that day? In Tuscany, we approach a meal from the other direction—we go to the market, see what looks the best, and plan our meal around these things.

When we shop for clothes or other items, we enjoy walking the streets, looking at things, choosing slowly and carefully. When it looks good or feels right, we know it. If you can transfer this attitude to food, you will discover something lost to people for a long time—or something new that many people have never known: the freedom and pleasure of shopping for food without a plan.

Don't buy food that comes in plastic, already cut up. Instead, shop where you can touch the vegetables, look at them; where you can see the fish as it comes from the sea—its color, the gills, the eyes—and smell it to see if it's fresh. It's nice to discover this way of shopping, which adds pleasure to how you think and feel about preparing a meal.

And forget about amounts and cooking times when you use this book. I'll help you understand that in your own kitchen you have all the freedom in the world to do exactly what you want, and the best way to arrive at solutions is through common sense.

For example, when you make a broth or a soup for four people, you know what size pan is required. You're not going to use a ten-gallon pot to make soup for four, and you're not going to use a teapot to prepare soup for twenty. So start with a pan big enough to hold all the ingredients for the number of people you want to serve, and that will help you decide the quantity of ingredients you need to buy.

You'll also know from the name of the recipe which ingredients are going to dominate the dish, so buy more of that ingredient. You know if you're making soft-shell crab soup that the main ingredient is crabs. The taste and whole personality of the dish is determined by how one or two ingredients dominate the others, but even these proportions can be varied. In Tuscan cooking, you never find a cook who tells you, "This *is it, this is the only way to make this dish." Instead, you always hear, "This is the way we make it; this is one of the ways we enjoy it." If you cook according to your own impulse, probably you will discover something about the way you like to cook.*

*Don't think that if you're given exact quantities and cooking times everything will turn out better. Sometimes it's the level of heat you use or the size of the pan that changes a dish. In between starting and finishing the dish, there are so many decisions you can make that if you follow a recipe given in table-*spoons and minutes you'll just lose your freedom.*

And, finally, I don't give exact times for cooking, either. Instead, I give an approximate time to start checking the dish to see if it's done. Why? First, an exact time doesn't exist. Second, there is a way to understand when food is ready that has nothing to do with the clock. Look at what's in the pan. See if it's getting too dry; smell it, penetrate it with a fork to see how tender it is. If you notice that it's a little too pink, cook it some more. If it's too dry, add more liquid. It's logical.

Canning, Tuscan-style

GLI ANTIPASTI

HUMBLE BEGINNINGS

By the time the legendary brigante *Tiburzi* died in the early 1900s he had killed more people than wild boars. I remember hearing the story of his capture when I was a boy. One day when he was trying to escape from the police, he asked for hospitality at a farmhouse in the hills near Pitigliano. The family agreed to provide Tiburzi with a loaf of freshly made bread, garlic, and some olive oil. This was the best that they could offer him for the long days ahead in the hills. But after his farewell at their door, Tiburzi realized he was surrounded by the military police and it would be impossible for him to escape. "Then forget it," he said. "Let them wait. Let's have the fettunta now and share my last taste of freedom." He took his time at the table with the family, and when he finished, he opened the door of the farmhouse, lifted his rifle, and . . . he had decided to die. The family who hid him were proud to tell all the people around of the courage Tiburzi showed after they shared his last meal with him.

Because Tiburzi had been such a criminal, the bishop of the city refused to let him be buried in consecrated ground. So they dug his grave at the outer edge of the cemetery so that his legs and body, which were not responsible for his crimes, would be in sacred land, but his head would not. They put a wild boar's head on the top of his grave and wrote on the gravestone, "Here finally rests the criminal Tiburzi."

Tiburzi was only 5'4" and 180 pounds, with a nice beard and a smiling face. He looked like a sweetheart, this guy who killed so many people.

Tiburzi was a very terrible and cruel man, but only to the rich landowners of Maremma. He was blackmailing them: "If you pay me, I won't rob you, or take your animals, or destroy your fields, and I'll make sure no one else does. But if you don't pay me, I will destroy everything you have." That's the kind of law that Tiburzi established in that area. At that time, and still today, when you kidnap someone, you want to hide them in Tuscany, in the area between Florence and Grosseto, because it is very wild and there are so many caves in the woods. And you want to be sure to have a shepherd in on it. The shepherds know those places better than the insides of their own pockets. One usually pictures shepherds standing around doing nothing, but not these guys. During the day they watch the animals, but at night they kidnap people. Kidnapping was a very popular activity in Italy in the nineteen seventies. It was a nighttime job; daytime, back to the goats.

Preceding pages: **Briganti and gendarmi**

FETTUNTA

TOASTED GARLIC BREAD

Through history, parts of Tuscany have been overrun by bandits, floods, the government, and the papacy. Peasants knew what it meant not to have food—to have only bread to eat for days and weeks and months. In the early part of the century, the peasants went on a general strike to protest their treatment by the wealthy landowners. They just stopped working, all of them. It was probably during this period that Fettunta (in Tuscany, a slice of toasted garlic bread, wet with oil) was invented as the only way to survive the months of food shortages.

One thing the peasants had was flour, so they made a very simple bread of flour and water. The other thing they had was a very heavy, unfiltered olive oil, which the rich people, with their refined tastes, rejected. In the beginning, Fettunta was simply bread brushed with olive oil and salt, and then toasted. Then the peasants started to add garlic and, once in awhile, some tomatoes. The big difference is that today we make Fettunta to enjoy it, but at that time the peasants made it to survive.

You can't make Fettunta with presliced, plastic-wrapped bread. You have to use simple white Italian bread with a good crust.

PANTRY	COLD STORAGE	MARKET
Olive oil	Garlic	Good Italian bread, sliced
Salt		
Black pepper		

Toast the bread and scrape a clove of garlic over one side of each slice. As you scrape, the garlic will disintegrate and release its pulp and juice into the bread. Sprinkle bread with olive oil.

In your home, it's nice if you serve plain toasted bread and on the table put cloves of garlic, a bottle of good olive oil, and salt and pepper. Each person scrapes as much garlic as he or she wants over the toasted bread and then puts on the olive oil, salt, and pepper.

FETTUNTA AL POMODORO
BREAD WITH TOMATOES

When I was a kid, this was one of my favorite snacks. I would eat it with stracchino cheese, which is very light. You have to make this with really juicy, ripe tomatoes; beefsteaks are the best. If you like, put some anchovies or oregano on top. This is a Fettunta, even though the bread isn't toasted and it doesn't have garlic.

PANTRY	COLD STORAGE	MARKET
Salt		Fresh tomatoes
Black pepper		Italian bread, sliced
Olive oil		Oregano (fresh, if available; optional)
Anchovies (optional)		

Rub the cut side of a tomato on a thick slice of bread. When all the juice is absorbed, put a little salt and pepper and olive oil on top, then anchovies or oregano, if you wish. This is excellent for a snack or for lunch accompanied with fresh mozzarella and basil.

FETTUNTA ALLE VONGOLE
FETTUNTA WITH CLAMS

When you're buying clams, remember that the shells weigh a lot, so get enough clams so that once they are out of the shell, you will have plenty to cover about four Fettunta.

PANTRY	COLD STORAGE	MARKET
Olive oil	Garlic, smashed	Cherrystone, Littleneck, or Manilla clams, cleaned
Salt		
Black pepper		
Fettunta (page 43)		

Prepare Fettunta as described. Put a clove of garlic and a few drops of olive oil in the bottom of a deep pan. Add clams, cover, and steam until their shells open. Discard any that haven't opened. Remove clams from shells, reserving clam broth, and chop them finely. Put them in a bowl with a very small amount of their own liquid and season them with salt, pepper, and a bit of olive oil. Spoon this mixture onto each slice of Fettunta and run under the broiler briefly to warm—just a few seconds. Top with a little olive oil before serving.

VARIATION To make FETTUNTA ALLE VONGOLE CON POMODORO (Fettunta with Clams and Tomato), spoon a layer of chopped fresh tomatoes on the garlic toast before adding the clams.

CROSTINI AL POMODORO

TOASTED BREAD WITH CHOPPED TOMATO

PANTRY	COLD STORAGE	MARKET
Olive oil	Garlic, minced almost to a paste	Fresh, very ripe tomatoes, peeled and chopped in tiny pieces
Salt		
Black pepper		Fresh basil, chopped (optional)
		Good Italian bread, thinly sliced

Place the tomatoes in a bowl. Moisten them with olive oil and sprinkle with salt and pepper to taste. Add basil if you wish. Set aside. Now mix the garlic into some olive oil and brush each slice of bread with this flavored oil. Toast on both sides until the edges of the bread begin to brown. Top with a spoonful of the tomato mixture and serve.

CROSTINI DI FEGATO DI CACCIA

GAME LIVER CROSTINI

PANTRY	COLD STORAGE	MARKET
Olive oil	Butter	Livers of duck, rabbit, goose, or any feathered game
Bay leaves	Salsa al Funghetto (page 98)	
Salt		Brandy
Black pepper		Fresh Italian bread, sliced
Ground coriander (optional)		
Fettunta (optional; page 43)		

Cook livers in butter and olive oil over high heat with bay leaves, salt, and pepper, and, if you wish, coriander. (I always add coriander, but some people don't like it. I use it because it sharpens the taste; it's like giving it an extra touch of perfume.) Once the livers are cooked, discard the bay leaves, finely chop the livers, and mix in a generous scoop of salsa and a splash of brandy. Season the mixture well. Livers have a tendency to be very sweet, so they need plenty of salt and pepper. Brandy also helps take away the sweetness and makes the livers taste sharper. Mix well and serve on bread or Fettunta.

CROSTINI ALLA FIORENTINA

CHICKEN LIVER PÂTÉ, FLORENTINE STYLE

My godfather was 100 percent Florentine, like the fifty generations before him. His wife used to make chicken liver crostini, and I remember asking him, "Why, when we have this at your house, is the bread so soft? It's different from the crostini of my mother." He told me that in Florence they soften the bread in hot chicken broth before they put the pâté on top. If you dip hard bread in broth quickly, just long enough to moisten it, it doesn't get mushy or fall apart. This is a Florentine way of using stale bread. In Florence they say, "Let the bifolchi do things their way and we'll do things our way." Florentines—always snobs. Bifolchi is the old Tuscan word for "peasant."

I love this recipe because I love sharp tastes. Have this beautiful crostini with a slice of prosciutto and a bottle of fresh, young white wine, still sparkling a bit. Find a patio overlooking Florence, sit down, and forget about the rest of the world.

PANTRY	COLD STORAGE	MARKET
Olive oil	Butter	Chicken livers (1 per person)
Capers, finely chopped	Chicken broth	Fresh Italian bread, sliced
Anchovies, finely chopped	Fresh parsley, chopped (optional)	
Salt		
Black pepper		

Sauté chicken livers over medium heat in equal amounts of butter and olive oil. Chop well, mix with capers and anchovies, and season with salt and pepper. Return to the pan and stir in a very little broth. Purée everything until it is the consistency of a thick paste. Serve warm or at room temperature on fresh bread. Sprinkle chopped parsley over the top if you want.

CROSTINI CON PORCINI ALLA GIANCARLO

GIANCARLO'S GARLIC BREAD WITH PORCINI

PANTRY	COLD STORAGE	MARKET
Olive oil	Red onion, chopped	Fresh porcini (see Note), chopped
Canned tomatoes, smashed in their own juice		Fresh Italian bread, sliced
White wine		
Anchovies		
Fettunta (optional; page 43)		

Heat some olive oil in a pan and sauté porcini and onion together over medium heat until the mushrooms release their water. Add some tomato, white wine, and an anchovy or two. Turn up the heat and cook until the liquid is reduced. Serve hot or at room temperature on fresh bread or Fettunta.

N O T E If you have on hand Salsa al Funghetto (page 98) made from porcini stems, you can use that instead of fresh porcini.

UOVA AL TARTUFO

EGGS WITH TRUFFLES

*T*uscans don't have any interest in a large, American-style breakfast. We believe the stomach needs respect in the morning, so the Italian breakfast is usually eggless. But as an antipasto at lunch or dinner with truffles, the egg is elevated to a more noble stature.

PANTRY	COLD STORAGE	MARKET
Salt	Eggs	Black or white truffles
Black pepper	Butter	

Fry eggs in butter, sunny side up. Thinly slice truffle on top. Season to taste with salt and pepper and serve.

FRITTATA DI CARCIOFI

ARTICHOKE FRITTATA

PANTRY	COLD STORAGE	MARKET
Olive oil	Lemon juice	Artichokes
Salt	Eggs	
Black pepper	Milk	

Cut off the top and stem of each artichoke and break off the hard outer leaves until you reach the soft, yellowish inside leaves. Cut artichokes into quarters and drop them into water to which lemon juice has been added. When all the artichokes are prepared, boil them until tender.

In a large pan, pour in enough oil so the artichokes will be able to swim in it. Heat oil until hot but not sizzling, then sauté artichokes over medium heat just until their color deepens. Drain on paper towels and allow them to return to room temperature.

Meanwhile, beat the eggs with salt, pepper, and a little milk until light and frothy. Moisten the bottom of a pan with olive oil. Put the artichokes in the pan and, over medium heat, pour the egg mixture over them. Let the egg mixture seep to the bottom, lifting the edges of the frittata as it cooks so the uncooked egg mixture on top seeps down. When the top of the frittata isn't liquid anymore but still uncooked, cover the pan with a plate and flip the frittata upside down onto the plate. Slide it back into the pan and cook on the other side, still over medium heat, until it is firm but still moist. Cut into wedges and serve hot or at room temperature as an appetizer.

FRITTATA DI MELANZANE

EGGPLANT FRITTATA

*I choose an eggplant by grabbing it in my hand. If it feels comfortable—
no bigger and no smaller than my hand, then it's the right one. It must
be very dark burgundy in color, with no spots, and very soft to the touch,
almost like velvet. Tuscans don't peel eggplant. The eggplant has a sweet
taste and the skin is the only bitter part. The sweet and bitter tastes balance
each other.*

PANTRY	COLD STORAGE	MARKET
All-purpose flour	Eggs	Eggplant
Corn oil	Milk	
Olive oil		
Salt		
Black pepper		

Remove the stem and cut the unpeeled eggplant lengthwise into thin slices.
Lightly dust each slice with flour and remove excess by shaking the slices in
a strainer. Sauté until golden in hot, but not sizzling, corn oil over medium
heat. Drain on paper towels and allow the slices to return to room temperature. Cut the slices in half and put them in a pan that you have rubbed with
a little olive oil.

   Beat the eggs with salt, pepper, and milk until light and frothy. Pour the
eggs into the pan and, over medium heat, let the mixture seep to the bottom, lifting the edges of the frittata as it cooks so the uncooked egg mixture
on top seeps down. When the top of the frittata isn't liquid anymore but is
still uncooked, cover the pan with a plate and flip the frittata upside down
onto the plate. Slide it back into the pan and cook on the other side, still
over medium heat, until firm but still moist. This can be served as an
appetizer.

PASTICCIO DI DANTE

DANTE'S SWEET MESS

Pasticcio *means plenty of sweet trouble. In* The Divine Comedy, *Dante made his own "pasticcio." With no intention of being fair, he put some people in hell and some others in paradise. So to me, Pasticcio di Dante is a mixture of ingredients so far apart that you think if you combine them you would end up with a mess. But the result is excellent. Pasticcio di Dante is a combination of capers, anchovies, and peppers: capers come from dry desert areas, anchovies come from the sea, and peppers are a cultivated product that comes from your garden. They don't sound as if they could work together, but try them and you'll see. I've eaten tons of this by the spoonful but I suggest you dip slices of crusty Italian bread into the pasticcio.*

PANTRY	COLD STORAGE	MARKET
Olive oil		Red, yellow, and green sweet peppers (any combination), seeded and cut lengthwise into slivers
Black pepper		
Capers, drained		
Anchovies, drained		Fresh Italian bread

Preheat the oven to medium hot. Heat olive oil over medium heat in an ovenproof pan. Add peppers and cook over high heat until they become limp. Discard excess liquid, season with pepper, and add the capers and anchovies. Cook over medium heat until anchovies are completely melted into the mixture.

Place the pan in the oven and let pepper mixture cook, uncovered, until the peppers look and smell roasted, and have dried out a bit. Be sure to turn them over 2 or 3 times so they don't burn. Serve warm or at room temperature with crusty fresh bread.

PROSCIUTTO E FICHI

PROSCIUTTO AND FIGS

This recipe is considered an appetizer, but actually it's the kind of dish you can eat any time. It is important to know how to choose the figs. If you want to eat them right away, the bottom part has to be soft. If they are what we call white figs, which are really very light green, they must not have any milky substance seeping out the top. If you like red figs, they must be as dark as possible—the darker the skin, the riper the fig—though softness is the most important indication.

Choose prosciutto according to your own taste, but with figs I suggest something very sweet, tender, and tasty—any prosciutto made in the northeastern part of Italy. There should be a good percentage of fat on the side of the prosciutto itself. It's nice to see a slice of two thirds lean meat and one third fat on the top. Be wary of prosciutto that is totally lean. Most of the time that means the prosciutto is made industrially and the aging is technologically controlled. Hand-cut prosciutto is always the best if you can get it.

Cut the figs in quarters and serve them on a bed of prosciutto. (You can peel the figs or leave the skin on.) The only seasoning I suggest is freshly ground black pepper—nothing else.

PLEBEIAN BEANS

No matter how humble you might have thought beans were, if you prepare them the way we do in Tuscany, you will change your mind. Tuscans love beans! In Italy, they call Tuscans "bean-eaters."

In the fall, we use dried beans cooked and combined in many different ways. Dried beans are one of the friendliest foods you can have in your house; they don't take up much space, and you can keep them on the shelf for months and take them out when you want them. Even after you've cooked them, they will stay in the refrigerator for at least a week—or until they get impatient and start to fizz.

In the summer, some varieties of beans are eaten fresh and sometimes raw. At that time of year they are so fresh you can still taste the minerals from the earth they grew in, and it would be a shame to cook them. The end of the summer is the end of their life again, all winter long.

Once you boil dried beans, they're good in everything: as an antipasto, in a simple salad, or as the complement to a main dish. Beans go well with every kind of bird—quail with beans, grouse or woodcock with beans. Delicious! Rabbit goes well with beans, too. So does red snapper.

Sometimes I mix different kinds of beans to make soup. I boil them separately, and then put them with tomatoes, broth, or whatever I feel like. I also make stew with beans.

Different beans are interchangeable in all dishes except salads. The black turtle beans taste much richer than the white, so they are too strong to be used in salads.

Although the bean dishes in this book belong to traditional Tuscan cuisine, you can always use your imagination and personal taste to change and combine them in different ways.

INSALATA DI FAGIOLI

BEAN SALAD

You can make a bean salad with chick-peas, cannellini beans, or lentils. No matter which bean you choose, always add oil and vinegar and salt and pepper. You can stop there, and they're delicious; or you can add other chopped vegetables. When I use chick-peas or cannellini beans, I add thin slices of red onion to sharpen the taste. If I want an even stronger taste, I add the white parts of scallions, sliced into tiny wheels. Sometimes I add celery, fennel, or parsley. If you don't like onions, leave them out entirely and add only the other vegetables—any or all of them.

As for the lentils, keep them simple. Scallions and lentils make a perfect marriage. They don't like a ménage à trois.

PANTRY	COLD STORAGE	MARKET
Chick-peas, cannellini beans, or lentils, soaked in water overnight	Red onions, chopped (optional)	Fennel, chopped (optional)
Olive oil	Celery, chopped (optional)	Scallions (white part), chopped (optional)
Salt	Fresh parsley, chopped (optional)	
Black pepper		
Red wine or balsamic vinegar		

No matter what combination you choose, put the dish together in the same way. Cook the beans until tender, then drain and add olive oil. (Some people like the beans swimming in oil, others like to pour in only enough to coat the beans and make them shine.) Now add salt and pepper to taste, then add other vegetables. If you decide to add the vegetables, start with a small amount, then add more, depending on how much you want the flavor of the vegetables to dominate the flavor of the beans. Add the vinegar splash by splash, drop by drop, to your personal taste. This is the final touch; to me, always the most important. You splash, you mix, you taste. When it's right for you, stop. If you think it needs more, add another drop of vinegar.

A generous spoonful of each of these bean salads on the same plate makes a nice combination. Somehow the tastes are distinctive enough to complement each other. Any of them can be served with a good cheese, some Italian salami or prosciutto, and a glass of good wine.

FAVE CON PECORINO

RAW FAVA BEANS WITH SHEEP'S MILK CHEESE

*O*ne *of the first signs of summer is the appearance of fava beans in the market. The first beans of the season are young, sweet, and tender enough to be eaten raw.*

Pecorino and caciotta are the same cheese at different ages. Tuscan caciotta is a fresh, young sheep's milk cheese. Pecorino is made with sheep's milk too, but it has been aged and is sharper. Caciotta is fresh and soft for about twenty-five days, and then it begins to form a hard crust. Once it reaches two months of age, it becomes a pecorino.

I like caciotta with fava beans; pecorino is also good, but if the fava beans are the tiny delicate ones that appear early in the season you may not want to serve them with too sharp a cheese.

PANTRY	COLD STORAGE	MARKET
Olive oil		Young, early fava beans
Salt		Pecorino or caciotta cheese, cubed
Black pepper		

Shell the beans and place in a bowl with the pecorino or caciotta, approximately 3 parts beans to 1 part cheese. (These cheeses are even sharper than Parmesan, so taste as you add.) Moisten well with olive oil and season to taste with salt and pepper. Be generous with the salt.

I FUNGHI

THE

JEWELS

OF

THE

WOODS

There is always a day in September when you go to sleep in the summer and you wake up in the fall. When you go to sleep it's kind of humid; you feel some rain in the air. And in the morning when you wake, the air is very clean—you can feel its sting. It's fresh but still warm. Your skin may still be black from the sun, but your spirit is moving toward autumn. You begin to think about what the new season may have to offer.

If you're lucky, Mother Nature has given you a beautiful fall starting very warm and slowing down, like spring backwards. There's a feeling that something is dying, but with style. Fall is very silent; it dies with discretion.

It's an injustice to say that everything dies in the fall and is born again in the spring. In all this death in nature, something is born in the fall—mushrooms! They may be one of the most precious things nature gives us. She seems to be saying, "Look at this. I'm going to be giving you six months of hard times, so enjoy this gift at the last moment."

Because mushrooms are seasonal and Tuscans love them so much, the tendency is to eat as many as you can while they're around. They are a celebration of the season, an event. When it's late summer or early fall in Tuscany and the porcini are in season, you will see them being sold on the street. Restaurants, vegetable markets, and trattorias have them displayed at their entrances. Because they are such celebrities, the whole meal is often dedicated to them.

Mushrooms taste great on their own but also are complementary to many other dishes. They can be grilled and served as an antipasto, sautéed and added to pasta, or cooked with meat in a stew for a main course. When mushrooms are in season, you want to eat them in as many ways as you can think of.

Mushrooms deserve great respect and attention. They don't want to be squeezed between menus and other dishes. That's why we've given them a chapter of their own.

FUNGHI CREMINI ALLA GRIGLIA

GRILLED CREMINI MUSHROOMS

Cremini (prataioli or brown mushrooms) are very popular in all of Italy. They are a poor cousin of the porcini (page 64). Cremini are in the market all year long, so they're the consolation when the porcini season is over. But remember, they're still a compromise. They look like poor porcini —a huge hat but more rounded and lighter in color. Like porcini, they cannot be washed in water. Cremini are very good served with a slice of prosciutto or salami. Cremini are the kind of mushroom that needs some help, and the help is always some kind of pork. This is not a fancy dish, but it's very, very good.

PANTRY	COLD STORAGE	MARKET
Olive oil		Cremini mushrooms
Salt		
Black pepper		

Wipe the cremini clean with a damp cloth. Separate the caps and stems. Slice stems. Sprinkle caps and stems with olive oil, salt, and pepper. Place them on a hot grill or under the broiler. Pierce mushroom pieces with a fork to see if they're tender after about 3 minutes. Turn mushrooms over and grill on the other side for 1 or 2 minutes. They are ready when they have lost excess water but are still somewhat firm. Toss with extra olive oil and serve.

INSALATA DI CREMINI

SALAD OF CREMINI MUSHROOMS

*T*his is a recipe you can make with any of the mushrooms with large, very firm caps. Use only balsamic vinegar here—you need the sweetness to balance the earthy flavor of the mushrooms.

PANTRY	COLD STORAGE	MARKET
Crushed red pepper	Garlic, very finely chopped	Cremini mushrooms, cleaned and sliced
Salt	Fresh parsley, chopped	
Olive oil		
Balsamic vinegar		

If you plan to bake the mushrooms, preheat the oven to medium. Bake or broil the mushroom slices with nothing on them. Check for tenderness in about 5 minutes. In the meantime, combine the other indredients for salad dressing. While the mushrooms are still warm, moisten them with dressing and mix well.

FUNGHI IN PADELLA CON ACETO BALSAMICO

SAUTÉED MUSHROOMS WITH BALSAMIC VINEGAR

*B*lack or white chanterelles, morels, shiitakes, pleurotes, golden oak mushrooms, or cultivated mushrooms are all suitable for this recipe. Oyster mushrooms can be prepared the same way, but without the balsamic vinegar. They are such a simple mushroom, the less done to them, the better.

PANTRY	COLD STORAGE	MARKET
Olive oil	Garlic, smashed	Fresh wild mushrooms (or cultivated, if wild are unavailable), cleaned and sliced
Salt	Fresh parsley, chopped	
Black pepper		
Balsamic vinegar		

In a pan, heat olive oil and sauté garlic over medium heat until full of color. Remove garlic, add mushrooms, and cook over high heat until they have absorbed the oil. Lower the heat, add salt and pepper to taste, and cook for a few minutes, stirring, until mushrooms release their juice. Remove from heat, pour off any excess liquid, and add balsamic vinegar to mushrooms, splash by splash, drop by drop, until it suits your taste. Correct seasoning, sprinkle with parsley, and serve at room temperature.

FUNGHI TRIFOLATI

WILD MUSHROOMS SAUTÉED
A DIFFERENT WAY

These two methods of preparing mushrooms work very well with white trumpet mushrooms, pleurotes and white or black chanterelles—the ones Tuscans call trombe di morto, or gallinacci. Once they are cooked, you can serve the mushrooms on a plate with bresaola (Italian air-dried beef), prosciutto, smoked breast of duck, Polenta (page 87) or Fettunta (page 43).

PANTRY	COLD STORAGE	MARKET
Olive oil	Garlic, smashed	Wild mushrooms
Salt	Fresh parsley, chopped	
Black pepper		
Anchovies (optional)		

Clean the mushrooms well, then prepare them in one of two ways: either sauté them over medium heat in olive oil with garlic until tender, then season with salt and pepper; or broil them in a flat pan with a little salt, pepper, and olive oil.

If all you have are cultivated mushrooms, pour some olive oil into a pan and add some smashed garlic and a couple of anchovies. Cook over medium heat until the garlic is golden and the anchovies have melted into the oil. Remove the garlic, add the thinly sliced msuhrooms, and sauté, still over medium heat. Serve, sprinkled with parsley and salt.

FUNGHI MISTI
CON PROSCIUTTO

MIXED WILD MUSHROOMS WITH PROSCIUTTO

Funghi Misti can be made with black or white chanterelles, shiitake, pleurotes, hen of the woods—anything that is available at the market. You can mix two or three varieties and serve them with a good companion like prosciutto, bresaola (Italian air-dried beef), salami, fresh or smoked mozzarella, or carpaccio (thinly sliced raw filet mignon).

PANTRY	COLD STORAGE	MARKET
Olive oil	Garlic, smashed	Several types of fresh wild mushrooms, cleaned
Salt		
Black pepper		Prosciutto, thinly sliced

Sauté the garlic in olive oil over medium heat until golden, then remove it. Add the mushrooms and sauté over high heat until they give up their liquid. Pour out any excess liquid, add salt and pepper, and continue to sauté the mushrooms until they reach the tenderness or crunchiness that you want. Serve on a bed of prosciutto.

MORCHELLE RIPIENE
CON BRESAOLA

STUFFED MORELS WITH BRESAOLA

PANTRY	COLD STORAGE	MARKET
Olive oil	Potatoes	Morels—4 or 5 per person as an appetizer
Salt	Garlic, chopped	
Black pepper	Fresh parsley, chopped	Bresaola (Italian air-dried beef), thinly sliced
	Egg yolks	
	Parmesan cheese	

If you plan to bake the morels, preheat the oven to hot. Choose good, plump morels with cavities big enough to stuff. Wipe them clean with a damp cloth and set aside.

Peel the potatoes, boil them, then chop them. Mix in some chopped garlic, chopped parsley, and enough egg yolk to bind the ingredients together, then add a bit of Parmesan cheese and salt and pepper to taste. Stuff the caps of the morels with this mixture. Put stuffed caps in a flat pan, sprinkle with olive oil, and bake or broil for no more than 3 to 5 minutes. Serve very hot, on a bed of bresaola. The tastes complement each other.

CAPPELLE DI FUNGHI RIPIENE

STUFFED MUSHROOM CAPS

I like to use cremini, shiitake, or cultivated mushrooms for stuffing. The caps must be well shaped and comfortable inside so that when you take the stems off, you have an alcove large enough for the stuffing.

PANTRY	COLD STORAGE	MARKET
Olive oil	Garlic, chopped	Eggplant, peeled and minced
Salt		Mushroom caps, large enough for stuffing, stems minced
Black pepper		Prosciutto, minced

Heat the olive oil in a pan and sauté the garlic over medium heat until golden. Remove garlic and add eggplant. You may not use the entire eggplant; you want equal amounts of eggplant and mushroom stems. Cook the eggplant over medium heat until tender, tossing frequently and adding small amounts of oil as needed to prevent sticking. Add mushroom stems and prosciutto, and cook the mixture several minutes over low heat until the flavors combine. If there is excess liquid, pour it off. Season with salt and pepper and stuff the mixture into the caps. Place caps on an oiled baking sheet and drizzle olive oil over the mushrooms. Bake in a moderate oven until the caps can be pierced easily with a toothpick.

I PORCINI

Of all the gems of the woods, the porcini are the crown jewels. You can find porcini when the rain begins at the end of summer. It's the first rain of August that calls them out, and once it begins, Tuscans who live in the country have only one thing in mind: the porcini are coming. You find the mushrooms hiding in the woods under the leaves and next to the big trees. The best ones are under the chestnut trees.

This is also the season when the poisonous snakes we call vipere deposit their eggs in the branches of the trees. When you're on your hands and knees searching for porcini, a viper can drop down and land on the back of your neck. You have to carry snakebite serum because if you're bitten, you have only minutes left to live.

One day I saw something so scary I thought I would never go hunting for porcini again. A friend and I were walking out of the woods into a field where the wheat had been cut to a stubble and the stems burned to fertilize the earth. We saw a peasant working there and, just as we approached, he was bitten on two fingers by a viper. He looked around, smiled, put the fingers on a piece of wood, took up his axe, and cut off the fingers. Then he wrapped his hand with a rag and walked slowly away. All I could think of was that the same thing could happen to me while hunting for porcini. All that for porcini? That's too much.

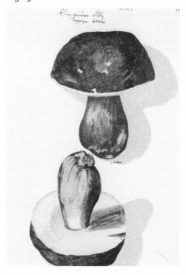

Porcini mushrooms

Some days later I saw the same man—without his two fingers, of course—still smiling as usual. He asked me if I was going for porcini, and I told him that after what I saw happen to him I had changed my mind. "Don't worry," he said. "If it's not a viper, it's going to be something else. If you like porcini, go after them. You want something good? You have to pay for it."

Usually when you hear about something like this, you think how cruel nature can be. But this man's reaction was a smile that meant, "That's life. Quit worrying about it."

Hunting season starts about the same time the porcini appear, and there are always people hunting for game on one side of the woods and people hunting for mushrooms on the other side. If the vipers don't get you, the hunters will. They see something move and they shoot. It happens all the time.

Once I saw a wild boar almost kill a hunter. It went after a man, and the only way he could save himself was to climb a tree. When his friends finally caught up with him, it took five blasts from a shotgun to kill the boar. When the incident was over and the hunters had moved the boar from where it had fallen at the base of the tree, all the man had to say was, "Damn it, that boar squashed all the porcini."

You can buy good porcini in most cities, but when you learn to find them in the woods, you can have them for free. Last fall I drove to a friend's house in upstate New York and parked the car in the yard under a plane tree. There I saw four beautiful porcini. Gorgeous. I just grabbed them, wrapped them in a piece of paper, put them in the car, and said, "Tonight I'll take care of of you." However, I wouldn't suggest that you do this unless you know mushrooms extremely well.

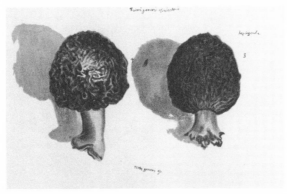

Morelle mushrooms

ABOUT PORCINI

CHOOSING PORCINI
Inspect the underside of the hat, which looks like a sponge and must be firm.

The stem should be fat and full of juice, so that when you feel it, you know it's a great, healthy porcini.

Porcini may vary in size. The color should always be dark brown with a very bright stem.

CLEANING PORCINI
Porcini, like all mushrooms, hate water. They have a tendency to get moldy right away. So never put them under running water or soak them.

Separate the hats from the stems and clean them carefully with a soft brush or a damp cloth. I know it's a pain in the neck, but it's worth it.

USING PORCINI The way to use porcini depends on their size. When the cap is 5 inches or more, just grill it. When you grill a mushroom, you are paying a compliment to its quality.

The stems and smaller porcini, like any mushroom, can be used in many different ways—for example, as a warm or cold appetizer or in a sauce.

The very small mushrooms, which are not as tasty, can be preserved in olive oil and taken out in the coldest months when you look around and can't even find a piece of rotten stone on the the ground.

DRIED OR FRESH? For me, there is only one kind of dried mushroom worth buying: porcini. Why? Because these mushrooms are very thick, juicy, and full of flavor. When you soak them in water or wine, they give back their good texture and taste. Experience has convinced me that dried morels, for example, are not even worth buying. They're such a woody mushroom when they're fresh, can you imagine what they're like after they've been dried? They become even more woody and lose their normal consistency and taste in the process. So except maybe for stews, stick with the porcini.

PORCINI ALLA GRIGLIA

GRILLED PORCINI MUSHROOMS

It's best to serve a grilled porcini alone, because its taste is so strong and so full of personality that it doesn't need any help. It's the most egocentric mushroom you can find. It doesn't want anything next to it on the plate. It's so meaty and mellow, it's considered like a steak in its taste and richness. The only thing I would serve with a grilled porcini is a great bottle of red wine. That's the obligation. Just sharpen your tongue, because the taste is unbelievable. I could eat porcini three times a day.

PANTRY	COLD STORAGE	MARKET
Olive oil		Fresh porcini mushrooms
Salt		
Black pepper		

Remove the caps of the mushrooms and reserve the stems for another use (see Using Porcini, preceding page). Lightly oil the caps and place them on a grill or in the broiler like upside-down umbrellas. When half cooked, they will feel spongy and release some water when you press them gently. Turn them over and continue to cook until tender but still firm. Drizzle with olive oil and season with salt and pepper.

ZUPPE E MINESTRE

THE

SOUPS

OF

BREAD

AND

FANTASY

Pasta and soup are eaten in every part of Italy, but in Tuscany, soup comes first in importance and then pasta. Soup appears on the table at least once a day and is considered as essential as any other course.

Tuscans like their soup rich and thick—with or without bread. Bread was the one element always present in the Tuscan kitchen, but fantasy raised a simple peasant soup to the level of culinary art. Bread may have filled the stomach, but Tuscan imagination provided the good taste. When the rich adapted these savory soups to their own tastes they eliminated the bread, which they didn't need, and substituted more of the other ingredients: fish, meat, and vegetables. Today when you eat a bread soup in Tuscany you know that you are eating an original peasant dish. But even if the soup is without bread, it will still represent the Tuscan approach of combining many flavors into one satisfying spoonful.

Page 68: *The Bean Eater* by Annibale Carracci

THE BREAD SOUPS

Credit for the following four soup recipes goes to my friend Donatella Cinelli. The last time I was in Tuscany, I asked her about the famous soups of Montalcino, and her face exploded into a big smile. Like all Tuscans, she wants to share information about her region so the food won't get lost and disappear forever. Even though I am living thousands of miles away, I still have in common with all the people of Tuscany the desire to keep alive what Tuscany is all about.

When I got back to New York, Donatella sent me a tiny book of soup recipes from a family diary that had been kept for generations on their estate in Montalcino. The following story, which she told me, gives a very real idea of the kind of people who once lived in that region.

During the twelfth century, when Florence and Siena were fighting each other in very bloody wars, the Montalcinesi were invited to step in on the side of the Sienesi. But the Montalcinesi managed to arrive when the confrontation was over, and the victorious Sienesi, to humiliate them, forced them to bury all the bodies of the Florentine soldiers who had died in battle. Today, seven hundred years later, if you tell someone in Siena that you come from Montalcino, he will call you a beccamorto—a gravedigger. The Montalcinesi will say, "We may have made a mistake once, but since then we have proved our courage in many other situations." There is a certain irony in this, because Tuscany is not a country that cares much about establishing a tradition of great warriors.

The Montalcinesi don't seem to mind being called gravediggers, as long as they are also known as good eaters and great wine producers. Like all Tuscans they like grilled poultry, red meat, and game—but, most of all, they like soup. These soups are examples of what people ate many years ago in the area of Montalcino, and they all have one thing in common: they are called zuppe di pane—the bread soups. Bread, a main ingredient, satisfied hunger, and the remaining ingredients provided good taste, moistness, and fragrance. These soups are thicker and richer than the liquid soups most people are used to.

ACQUACOTTA

ONION SOUP, MAREMMA STYLE

*T*his is a thick onion soup, flavored with tomatoes and herbs, and it gets better tasting the longer it's cooked. Like other recipes with "Maremma" in the title, it has a strong, sharp taste.

PANTRY	COLD STORAGE	MARKET
Olive oil	Garlic, smashed	Fresh mint and thyme or other herbs of your choice
Canned tomatoes, smashed in their own juice	Red onions, thinly sliced	Stale bread, cut in chunks
Salt		
Black pepper		

Heat the olive oil in a pan, add the garlic and onions, and sauté them over medium heat. Don't cook the onions all the way through; just let them get blond. Take out the garlic, add the tomatoes, salt, pepper, and herbs of your choice. Cook over high heat until mixture is hot and all the flavors have combined. Cover with cold water—3 times the amount of the other ingredients—then reduce the heat to low. Cook partially covered at least 1 hour—the longer the better. At the last minute, soak the chunks of bread in the soup and serve hot.

ACQUACOTTA DEI LOGAIOLI

GARDENER'S SOUP

Logaioli *were the people who took care of the vegetable gardens for the families that owned large estates in Tuscany. They lived in rustic houses in the hills, but to the people who only had bread and onions, the* logaioli *were privileged workers because their* dispensas *were loaded with all the produce from the rich landowners' gardens. They had such a large variety of vegetables that their wives invented a new soup every day. This is one of the most beautiful ones.*

PANTRY	COLD STORAGE	MARKET
Olive oil	Garlic, smashed	Fresh tomatoes, coarsely chopped
Crushed red pepper	Chicken or vegetable broth	Zucchini, coarsely chopped
Salt		Fresh or stale Italian bread, thinly sliced

Over high heat, sauté the garlic in olive oil along with the hot pepper and some salt. Add the tomatoes and sauté them until they are completely cooked. Reduce the heat to medium, add the zucchini, and continue cooking until all the vegetables are soft. Add a large amount of broth and bring to a boil, then reduce heat and cook, partially covered, for 20 to 25 minutes. Meanwhile, place 1 slice of bread in each bowl. When the soup is ready, pour it over the bread.

ACQUACOTTA
DEI BOSCAIOLI
WOODSMAN'S SOUP

*T*his is a very old recipe that came originally from the area of Maremma but became well known in Montalcino, which is in the hills only about thirty miles away. It has a very strong taste, and it suits our modern times. Even though people are more sophisticated now, they can still appreciate the austerity of this dish.

PANTRY	COLD STORAGE	MARKET
Olive oil	Red onions, finely chopped	Swiss chard leaves, coarsely chopped
Salt	Chicken or vegetable broth	Fresh or stale Italian bread, very thinly sliced
Black pepper		
Canned tomatoes, smashed in their own juice		

Sauté onions in olive oil over high heat, then add Swiss chard, salt, and pepper. Let the greens wilt, then add the tomatoes and enough broth to cover the ingredients. Bring the soup to a boil, then partially cover, and simmer 45 minutes to 1 hour. Meanwhile, put a slice of fresh or stale bread in each bowl and, when the soup is ready, pour it over the bread. Top with olive oil. You will see how simple it is, and how great this soup tastes.

ZUPPA DI CAVOLO
E PANE

CAULIFLOWER AND BREAD SOUP

This is considered one of the great soups of the Montalcino area. It is a bread soup with very little broth; it will look like a sloppy bread pudding. Serve the soup right away.

PANTRY	COLD STORAGE	MARKET
Salt	Garlic	Cauliflower
Olive oil	Parmesan cheese	Italian bread
Black pepper		

Remove the outside leaves from the head of the cauliflower and boil them in a large quantity of salted water for about 10 minutes. Coarsely chop the cauliflower into florets and add them to the pot. Cook at a low boil until completely tender. Drain the leaves and florets and keep the water they were cooked in—you're going to use it. Meanwhile, slice the bread, toast it, and rub both sides with garlic. Soak the bread in the cauliflower water.

Now start to build the soup. In a large bowl or individual bowls, make a layer of bread. Sprinkle it with olive oil, salt, pepper, and Parmesan cheese. Then spread a layer of cauliflower florets and leaves over the bread. Make another bread layer and keep building until you run out, working quickly so the soup stays hot. It's good cold, but it's great hot.

A VILLAGE CALLED
FEMMINA MORTA

My friend and I were driving one day from Florence to Lucca, when we saw a sign pointing the way to a town called *Femmina Morta. I was attracted more to the "woman" part of the town's name than the "dead" part, but neither of us could imagine what such a town would be like. We decided to find out.*

We wound our way through the hills until we reached a village of about fifty houses. It was lunchtime, and we found a tiny trattoria no more than twenty feet long, with an open kitchen so you could see everything that was going on. We loved it. We liked the idea of having a nice lunch in an unexpected place on a beautiful warm day in April

The owner was the classic trattoressa—*a big woman in her late fifties with a big smile, who smelled of a combination of dirt,* herbs, and garlic. This more than anything is the aroma I associate with the hill towns of Tuscany. She was making Ribollita, and she told us it had been cooking since early morning and would be ready soon. While we were waiting, we could have prosciutto, cheese, and something to drink. In these tiny villages you can get local wine or Campari. That's it. Drink wine.

Our table was next to an open door hung with colored streamers to keep the flies out. The soft spring breeze moving through the streamers created a curious sound that had a hypnotic effect on me. As I looked out an open window, I thought I was dreaming when a group of peasant girls carrying scythes appeared walking across a field. It seemed as if they were stepping out of a painting framed by my window.

As they came closer, I saw that

one of the girls was something that Mother Nature makes only once in a while: perfect harmony of beauty, sympathy, and energy. She was so beautiful that when she passed by the window I had to say something.

I asked her to join us for lunch, but she said she would have to ask her mother first. (I didn't want her mother involved because in Tuscany once the mother is involved it's all over. You have to go home, you have to introduce yourself, and they've got you from then on.) I told her that all I wanted was to look at her beautiful face while I was eating. After awhile—and this is what I love about a certain kind of Tuscan woman—she invented a reason to come into the trattoria.

When the trattoressa brought the Ribollita and a huge plate of scallions, the girl finally sat down and we began to eat in the traditional Tuscan way: a spoonful of Ribollita, then a bite of scallion dipped in salt. There was a difference, though, in the way she ate. She scooped out her soup with bread crusts instead of a spoon.

When she saw me watching her, this beautiful girl was embarrassed and said, "What's wrong? Do I look vulgar to you?" It was the other way around. Ribollita is a peasant dish, and her way of eating it was so simple and natural that my Florentine manners seemed pretentious.

"I've never eaten Ribollita with a metal spoon," she told me. "Metal spoons make the Ribollita taste tinny. When it's so good the way it is, why change it?" I put down my spoon and finished my soup in her style.

The town is still there. I don't know about Cecilia. She was the most unforgettable woman I've ever met. There are many beautiful women, but she was beauty and happiness and life—and the last thing I expected to find in a town named Femmina Morta.

RIBOLLITA

"OVERCOOKED" BREAD AND VEGETABLE SOUP

The Ribollita most often found in Tuscany includes beans and purple cabbage. The other vegetables vary according to the season and the mood of the cook. The following is the version I grew up with. Sprinkle extra olive oil in each bowl and serve the soup with raw, chilled scallions. A bite of scallion adds a sharp taste to each spoonful of soup.

PANTRY	COLD STORAGE	MARKET
Olive oil	Potatoes, cut in chunks	Zucchini, thinly sliced
Canned tomatoes, smashed in their own juice		Cauliflower, cut in pieces
Cannellini beans, partially cooked		Cabbage (white and purple), coarsely chopped
Salt		Swiss chard, chopped
Black pepper		Spinach
Odori (page 30)		Bread, cut in chunks

Heat the olive oil in a large pot and add the odori. Sauté over medium heat and, once the odori is soft, add the tomatoes, fresh vegetables, potatoes, cannellini beans, and just enough water to cover. Let them cook slowly until they are completely mushy. Season with salt and pepper. Take the soup off the heat, and add the bread and enough olive oil to flavor. Let the soup cool to allow the flavors to combine; it can even remain in the refrigerator overnight. Put the mixture back on the heat and let it cook slowly for at least 30 minutes. *Ribollita* means "overboiled," so it is impossible to cook this soup too long.

VARIATION ZUPPA MAREMMANA is similar to Ribollita, but the predominant ingredients are beans, zucchini, and potatoes, lots of herbs, very little spinach, and, like Ribollita, lots of bread. They're both cooked the same way; it's just how much you want one ingredient to prevail over the other.

PAPPA AL POMODORO

TOMATO AND BREAD SOUP

*T*his is the kind of dish that Tuscans eat all summer and late into the fall. No real Tuscan can escape eating this soup—like it or not. This soup looks like a red bread pudding.

PANTRY	COLD STORAGE	MARKET
Olive oil	Vegetable broth	Stale bread
Black pepper	Garlic, smashed	Fresh, ripe tomatoes, coarsely chopped
		Fresh basil, chopped

Soak the stale bread in a bowl of broth while you brown the garlic in olive oil over medium heat. Turn the heat up to high and add the tomato chunks —skin and all—to the pan. Cook over high heat, stirring slowly, and then add the basil. When the tomatoes have cooked for awhile and have a thick consistency, take the bread out of the broth with your hands and squeeze and shred it into the tomatoes and basil. Serve in warm bowls and toss with additional olive oil. Sprinkle generously with freshly ground black pepper, and that's it.

SOUPS WITHOUT BREAD

Soups made without bread are called minestre. They are made with more water than the bread soups, but with a large quantity of vegetables, which makes them as thick as the bread soups. Who knows? Maybe replacing the bread with vegetables was one of the early signs of future prosperity in Tuscany.

A nice minestrone is one of the most perfect dishes in the world. And, believe me, you can't make a mistake when you make vegetable soup unless you leave it on the stove for two days. Always use the freshest ingredients. You can make any ingredient more prevalent than another just by increasing the quantity. It depends on your taste.

Minestra di Verdure is basically a vegetable soup, a daughter of the Ribollita (page 78) but weaker. Make it the same way as Ribollita but without the bread. You can use potatoes, string beans, spinach, tomatoes, red beets, and peas, if you like. Cauliflower is good, too. Use any kind of vegetable; the only one you have to watch out for is celery. Don't ever use too much celery in any combination of vegetables because it makes everything taste acidic. The difference between the soups is in the amount of liquid. If you are making Minestra, once the vegetables are braised in the olive oil, cover them with cold water. Let the mixture cook very slowly for about 2 hours, and you'll have a simple, excellent vegetable soup with more liquid than Ribollita. You can add pasta if you want. It's called a zuppa without the pasta and a minestra with the pasta. You can use rice or penne, tubettini, spaghettini, or any kind of hard-wheat pasta. If the pasta is the wrong shape, break it into pieces. Serve the soup with Parmesan cheese sprinkled on top.

ZUPPA DI CECI

CHICK-PEA SOUP

PANTRY	COLD STORAGE	MARKET
Chick-peas, soaked in water overnight	Garlic, smashed	Prosciutto (see Note) with fat, chopped (optional)
Olive oil	Red onions, chopped	
Salt	Chicken or vegetable broth	Rosemary (fresh, if available)
Black pepper		
Pasta for *minestra:* cracked penne or tubettini (optional)		

Drain the chick-peas and boil in a pot of fresh water until tender. Mash half of them. Sauté the garlic in olive oil over medium heat until full of color. Remove garlic, add the onions, and cook over low heat until soft. Add mashed and whole chick-peas, then slowly stir in broth until the soup is thick. If prosciutto is to be added, do it now; it makes the soup much richer. Add salt, pepper, and rosemary and simmer, partially covered, until the flavors are well blended—about 30 minutes. If the soup gets too dry, add more broth. Broken, raw pasta may be added; then the soup becomes what Tuscans call a *minestra.* If you add pasta, add more broth and cook until the pasta is al dente. Sprinkle each serving with olive oil.

Some people like to sprinkle Parmesan cheese on the soup. I don't. Rosemary is very aromatic and doesn't go well with Parmesan. This soup can be served slightly chilled, but take it out of the refrigerator 30 minutes before serving.

NOTE Eliminate the salt in this recipe if you use prosciutto.

ZUPPA DI LENTICCHIE
LENTIL SOUP

PANTRY	COLD STORAGE	MARKET
Olive oil	Garlic, smashed	
Lentils, soaked in water overnight	Celery, finely chopped	
Long-grain Italian rice or pasta, a handful per person (optional)	Red onion, finely chopped	
Salt	Chicken or vegetable broth	
Black pepper	Parmesan cheese, grated (optional)	

Heat olive oil in a pan and sauté garlic over medium heat until golden. Remove garlic, add celery and onion, and cook until blond. Drain lentils, add them to the pan, and cook over low heat until the flavors combine, about 5 to 10 minutes. Add plenty of broth so that the lentils swim comfortably in the liquid. Bring to a slow boil, reduce the heat, cover, and let the mixture cook slowly until the lentils are tender. Cooking time may vary from 30 minutes to 1 hour, depending on the lentils. If you want a thicker soup, add rice or pasta. If adding rice, this should be done about 30 minutes before serving. Season the soup with salt and pepper and sprinkle each serving with Parmesan cheese if you like. To enhance the flavor, drizzle olive oil on top of each bowl of soup before serving.

PASTA E FAGIOLI

PASTA AND BEAN SOUP

PANTRY	COLD STORAGE	MARKET
Olive oil	Red onions, thinly sliced	Prosciutto, with fat and skin, cut into chunks
Black pepper	Tomato paste (optional)	Rosemary (fresh, if available)
Cannellini beans, soaked overnight and drained	Beef or chicken broth or water	
Wine, red or white		
Tubettini pasta		

Heat olive oil in a pan and sauté onions over medium heat until golden. Add the prosciutto and allow it to melt into the oil. When everything has had a chance to blend together, add the pepper and beans, mashing some of the beans into the mixture. Mix well and add a generous glass of wine. Add the rosemary—a small branch of fresh rosemary, if you can find it—and two soup spoons of tomato paste if you like. Cover the beans with broth or water, bring to a boil, then reduce heat to low and continue to cook, partially covered. When the beans start to get tender, take about half of them out of the pan, mash them, put them back in the pot, and continue to cook over low heat. The soup will have the thickness of the mashed beans and the texture of the whole beans. Take out the prosciutto—it has already flavored the soup—and, if you want, eat it. If the soup seems too thick, add more water. During the last few minutes of cooking, add broken pasta pieces. After about 30 minutes, when everything smells right, serve the soup with a little olive oil on top.

CACCIUCCO AI FUNGHETTI

MUSHROOM SOUP

*C*acciucco is the fish soup of the people living on the Tuscan coast, but people in the country living far from the sea manage to find their own imaginative way to make Cacciucco from something they have in great quantity. Instead of making it with fish, they make it with mushrooms. They combine simple mushrooms that never had much glory with other ingredients to generate a great soup. This soup can be made with any variety of mushrooms, and it is always good.

PANTRY	COLD STORAGE	MARKET
Olive oil	Garlic	Fresh mushrooms, coarsely chopped
Salt		
Black pepper		Fresh mint leaves, left whole
Canned tomatoes, smashed in their own juice		
Fettunta (page 43)		

Cover the bottom of a pan with olive oil, heat it, and add 2 or 3 cloves of garlic. Let the oil get very hot, then add all the mushrooms. Season with a little salt and pepper and add as many fresh mint leaves as you like—a good quantity because mushrooms and mint are a great combination. Cook over high heat for a few minutes, then add enough tomatoes to cover the mushrooms. Continue to cook over high heat for another 4 or 5 minutes, then add twice as much water as there are mushrooms and tomatoes. Let it reach the boiling point, reduce the heat, and simmer, partially covered, for 45 minutes to 1 hour. That's it; the soup's finished. Ladle into bowls in which have been placed a slice of Fettunta.

IL BUGLIONE

Civiltà Contadina Toscana. These words have a special meaning to Tuscans. Civiltà *is a noble word that stands for "respect and dignity," and* contadina Toscana *refers to the country people who work the land. This expression synthesizes the origins of Tuscan culture.*

The word civiltà *tells you that the peasants of Tuscany have always had the dignity to take a stand against misery, poverty, and disease and that they have had the imagination to put food on the table that was decent and good, even if it was only bread and whatever was available in their gardens or grew wild in the surrounding fields. Tuscans—whether they were in the countryside, worked the coal mines, or were poor fishermen—always found ways to make their simple meals pleasant.*

There is a dish in Tuscany called Buglione, which is very, very old but still served today. This dish was born in the flatlands of Siena and the lower area of Arezzo at a time when there were many castles and rich people (good for them) and many servants and poor people (bad for them—very, very bad). Sometimes the rich people were generous, and they gave away the feet and neck of the goose, the blood of the lamb, and all the other pieces and parts they didn't use because they were rich (good for them). The poor servants were forced to squeeze their brains to think of something to do with these leftovers.

This is how the peasants of Tuscany made Buglione. They boiled whatever pieces of meat they had, which could be parts of a chicken or lamb, the neck of a duck, the foot of a pig, tripe from a calf, and, if the rich people were really generous, maybe a piece of wild boar. When everything was half cooked, soft enough to separate the meat from the bones, they took the meat out of the broth and put it in another pot. They chopped onions, celery, carrots, and a little bit of garlic and added all the fresh herbs they could find in their area: catmint, thyme, sage, juniper berries. Then, using the best olive oil they had, they very slowly sautéed the odori and herbs until they were golden, then added them to the pot with the meat. They covered everything with water and let it boil slowly for so long that it became almost as smooth as cream. Once everything was very hot, it was put on top of Fettunta (page 43).

This is Buglione—a dish of many flavors and lots of imagination.

POLENTA: A MEAL
FOR MANY DAYS

As I've said before, bread has always been a major ingredient in a Tuscan meal. But Polenta, too, has been very important. Especially, in some northern parts of Tuscany, and even in certain parts of Maremma, they used to have a lot of cornmeal—and only that.

While the men went to work in the fields, the women of ancient Tuscany would prepare a dish called *La Polenta Incatenata*. When the women of Tuscany prepared this dish, it took them hours because it was almost a ritual. The broth had to be just right, made with the right ingredients; the onions had to be sliced a certain way; and the cabbage and beans had to be cooked slowly. Everything was done with care in the tradition of Tuscany.

The first meal of the Incatenata started with an excellent broth, which was made by boiling a good quantity of water with prosciutto bones or meaty pork bones. Cooking on the side were beans, purple cabbage sliced in strips, and potatoes cut in cubes. Once the vegetables were added to the broth, the women started stirring in the cornmeal until it reached the right consistency: thick but liquid, not firm. They would sauté tiny pieces of Italian bacon in olive oil along with parsley and rosemary, and this, too, was mixed into the Polenta. The whole dish was sprinkled with good extra-virgin olive oil and a bit of shredded cheese.

When the men came home at midday to eat, they had this soft cornmeal with a nice piece of bread to fill their stomachs. Whatever was left over would be set aside for the evening meal.

As the Polenta cooled, it became firm—as we say, rappresa. So at night, for dinner, it was sliced like bread, fried, and eaten very hot. This was the second meal of the Incatenata. Whatever was left from this meal would be saved and served to the children at breakfast the next morning, with a type of Livornese sauce—tomatoes with very little garlic.

Incatenata *stands for the chain of meals that Tuscan women could get out of one simple, poor dish. It is a good example of the heartbreaking imagination of the people of Tuscany.*

POLENTA

CORNMEAL MUSH, TUSCAN STYLE

In the late nineteenth century in Tuscany, there was a malaria epidemic in Maremma, and government officials in bordering areas were authorized to destroy food and burn shacks where people had died. If you look carefully at paintings of Tuscany showing peasant food before that time, you see bread on the table, but after that if you see something yellow in the middle of the table, it's usually polenta. Tuscany was so poor that bread became the food of the rich and polenta the food of the poor.

Polenta can be a substitute for pasta or bread. It can be soupy like cornmeal mush or stiff like cornbread. I make it the first way once in awhile for myself and eat it with sausage sautéed with tomatoes for another very strong dish. With a good bottle of wine, who's going to bother you? You're through for the day.

PANTRY	COLD STORAGE	MARKET

Yellow cornmeal

Salt

Black pepper

Bring a pot of water to a low boil. Add cornmeal to the boiling water a handful at a time by letting it sift through your fingers, stirring with your other hand as you do this. Keep stirring and adding cornmeal until the polenta reaches a consistency heavy enough to hold a wooden spoon upright in the pot. Add salt and pepper to taste. The consistency may vary according to the dish you are serving it with or your personal taste. You may like it firmer with a tomato sauce or, if you serve it with game, you may want it softer. If you have polenta with mushrooms or vegetables, which are more delicate, it is good almost runny.

PASTA E BASTA

PASTA, THAT'S ALL

My brothers and I would always come home from school starving to death, but we had to wait to eat until my father came home from work. When it grew late, my mother got hungry, too. We would sit at the table with empty plates in front of us and nothing to do while my mother stood at the window looking out at the street, waiting for my father. He would leave the car at the corner and walk the rest of the way to the house. One day we asked, "Mamma, what are you doing at the window?" And she said, "I'm looking for your father's shoes so I can throw the pasta in the water." When she saw the first bit of shoe come around the corner, she would put the pasta on, and by the time he got home the pasta was cooked to perfection—al dente.

Pasta needs to be cooked in plenty of fast-boiling water. There has to be enough water in the pot so the pasta can swim around freely. Add salt once the water is boiling. And before you start to make any sauce, have a pot of water boiling slowly nearby, so you can cook the pasta when the sauce is almost ready.

To judge whether the pasta is cooked enough, lift out one piece and break it with your fingernail. If it feels too hard, it's not cooked enough. You can test it the same way with your teeth; that is what we call al dente. When it feels pleasurable to the touch of your teeth, the pasta is ready—not too soft, not too hard, right in between.

In Italy, pasta breaks down all barriers and crosses all borders. Although we know that spaghetti and all the other hard-wheat pastas are a southern Italian invention, in Tuscany it's the sauce that counts— in perfect balance with the pasta, never overwhelming and never too runny but always original in taste.

Page 88: **Spaghetti vendors**   Above: **Spaghetti factory**

In Tuscan cooking, the sauces are incorporated into the pasta instead of remaining on top like a liquid garnish. To do this, we put the pasta and the sauce together in a different manner than do other Italians. Once the pasta is cooked, drain it and then add it very quickly to the pan that the sauce is in, while they are both hot. In this way, the pores of the pasta can absorb the taste of the sauce, and the flavor will spread throughout. If you are adding Parmesan, do it while everything is still in the pan, and toss. It will further tie the sauce to the pasta.

When you buy Parmesan cheese, always make sure you get a piece of the crust. First, the crust has the name of the cheese printed on it, and it tells you where it comes from. You don't want an industrially produced American Parmesan cheese, which lacks the texture and taste of the genuine product from Parma. Second, the crust is excellent grated and used in cooking or combined with the center of the cheese and grated on top of pasta. Just scrape the printing off with a sharp knife. Stores usually keep the crusts for themselves and sell them as ready-made grated cheese, but it's better if you combine the crust with the pulp and grate it yourself.

You don't have to keep Parmesan cheese in the refrigerator unless you're storing it for a long time. In my restaurant I dampen a piece of cheesecloth and wrap it around the cheese so it keeps the moisture inside. If you want to refrigerate the Parmesan, cover the damp cheesecloth with plastic wrap and it will stay indefinitely. But Parmesan cheese is not something you want to buy in large quantities. As soon as you taste it, you want to finish it. Who wants to refrigerate it?

Spaghetti lover

TAGLIATELLE AL SUGO D'AGNELLO

FRESH EGG NOODLES WITH LAMB SAUCE

PANTRY	COLD STORAGE	MARKET
Olive oil	Parmesan cheese, grated	Lamb, cut in chunks for stewing
Red wine		Thyme (fresh, if available)
Salt		Tagliatelle (fresh, if available)
Black pepper		
Canned tomatoes, smashed in their own juice		
Nutmeg		
Odori (page 30)		

Cover the bottom of a pan with olive oil and slowly warm it over low heat. Add the odori and continue to cook until soft. Mix in the lamb and cook until it turns white, making sure all the meat touches the olive oil and vegetables. Add a couple glasses of wine and turn up the heat to cook until the wine evaporates. Sprinkle with thyme, salt, and pepper and cook 5 to 10 minutes. Cover mixture generously with the tomatoes and season delicately with nutmeg. Continue to cook, uncovered, over high heat until boiling. Turn the heat down very low, cover, and continue to cook for 1½ to 2 hours, stirring frequently. The sauce will turn a very dark red. If the mixture gets too dry, add water.

When the sauce is ready, cook the tagliatelle until al dente in boiling water. Drain well and add to sauce. Sprinkle with Parmesan cheese, mix thoroughly, and serve with additional Parmesan on the side. Any remaining sauce can be stored in the refrigerator for several days; the flavor only improves.

TAGLIOLINI AL TARTUFO BIANCO O NERO

THIN EGG NOODLES WITH WHITE OR BLACK TRUFFLES

The most important characteristic of white truffles is their strong, aromatic smell. Black truffles have almost no scent, but their taste is even stronger than the white. White truffles are also more rare and expensive. This is a very seasonal dish. White truffle season is from the middle or the end of September until late November—the length of the season depends on the weather. Black truffles follow the whites in season—from December or January until the end of February.

PANTRY	COLD STORAGE	MARKET
Salt	Butter	Tagliolini (fresh, if available)
Black pepper	Parmesan cheese, grated	Fresh white or black truffles

Boil tagliolini in salted water until al dente. Melt a generous portion of butter in a large pan. When pasta is done, drain well and add to pan. Stir enough to lightly coat the tagliolini. Very quickly, thinly slice the truffles over the pasta, reserving some for garnish. Mix the butter, tagliolini, and truffles quickly, adding just a touch of Parmesan—go very easy on the Parmesan so it doesn't overwhelm the truffles. Season to taste with salt and pepper. The mixture doesn't have to cook; it only needs to be warmed through. Serve on a warm plate with additional truffle shaved over the top.

TAGLIATELLE ALL'ORTOLANA

FRESH EGG NOODLES WITH FLAVORS OF THE KITCHEN GARDEN

*A*ny *pasta can be used here except pappardelle—it's too thick. Penne or even spaghetti are all right. (I never use linguine in any recipe. Linguine is a southern Italian pasta that we don't use in Tuscany; we use round spaghetti.) This recipe is good year-round because the vegetables can be changed according to the season.*

In certain dishes, like this one, the vegetables need to be cut by hand. I always use a mezzaluna, *the half-moon–shaped knife, because I like to see the imperfections of the slices. When a machine is used for cutting, chopping, or slicing, the violent power inside the machine makes the vegetables fall apart and lose their consistency when they are cooked. They taste good enough, but the presence of the whole vegetable is gone.*

PANTRY	COLD STORAGE	MARKET
Olive oil	Red onions, chopped	Any combination of the following vegetables: fresh fava beans, eggplant, spinach, zucchini, asparagus, artichoke hearts, broccoli florets, carrots, Swiss chard, fresh tomatoes
Salt	Chicken or vegetable broth	
Black pepper	Parmesan cheese, grated	
	Butter (see Note)	Fresh herbs of your choice: mint, sage, oregano, parsley, basil
		Tagliatelle (fresh, if available)

Heat olive oil in a pan and sauté onions over medium heat until golden. When the onions are done, add the fava beans; eggplant, peeled and cut into bite-sized pieces; spinach, roughly cut; and zucchini, cut into bite-sized pieces. Season with salt and pepper, turn the heat to low, and continue to cook and stir until vegetables are tender but still crisp. If vegetables begin to dry out, add some broth. When almost cooked, add the asparagus, parboiled and cut into bite-sized pieces; artichoke hearts, steamed and quartered; broccoli florets, steamed; carrots, cut into ovals and steamed; or

Swiss chard, shredded and sauteed. Add just enough tomatoes to give some color, then add whatever herbs you are using.

Cook the pasta until al dente in boiling water and drain. Add to vegetables, along with the Parmesan cheese and butter. Mix thoroughly over low heat and serve with additional Parmesan cheese on the side.

N O T E Replace olive oil with butter throughout the preparation if you prefer a richer dish.

TAGLIATELLE CON PORCINI AL FUNGHETTO

FRESH EGG NOODLES IN WHITE PORCINI SAUCE

I once had this outside Florence, but the mushroom water was left in the pan instead of being cooked off and nepitella (catmint) was added to the water, which gave the dish a totally different taste.

PANTRY	COLD STORAGE	MARKET
Olive oil	Garlic, smashed	Fresh porcini stems
	Butter	Tagliatelle (fresh, if available)
	Parmesan cheese (grated)	

Cut the porcini stems lengthwise, in wheels, or diagonally. (I prefer diagonally because they look more pleasing.) Heat olive oil in a pan and sauté garlic over medium heat until golden. Remove the garlic, add porcini, and sauté quickly over medium heat until the mushrooms lose their water. Continue cooking until the liquid evaporates. Cook the pasta in boiling water until al dente. Drain well and add to pan along with a scoop of butter and some Parmesan. Mix thoroughly over low heat until the pasta is warmed through and has absorbed the taste of the sauce. Serve with additional Parmesan.

TAGLIATELLE AL SUGO DI CACCIA

FRESH EGG NOODLES WITH GAME SAUCE

You can save leftover parts of game and freeze them, either raw or cooked, for this dish. When you have collected enough, mix them and make the Sugo di Caccia.

For example, when I make medallion of venison, I use the saddle and save the leftovers. You can also do this with duck, pigeon, squab, rabbit, or quail. Save the liver and interiors, too. But if you don't want to go through the nuisance of collecting the parts of animals, or if you are sensitive about these things, just buy fresh game from a good butcher.

This sauce is my favorite. Wild meat is sweet and rich, and the olives give a little bit of sour taste. And the olives and thyme together help to bring out the sweetness of the meat.

PANTRY	COLD STORAGE	MARKET
Olive oil		Any combination of the following game: wild boar, antelope, venison, hare, pheasant, quail, partridge, squab, wild duck, goose
Bay leaves		
Red wine		
Canned tomatoes, smashed in their own juice		
Black olives, pitted and coarsely chopped		Thyme (fresh, if available)
Odori (page 30)		Tagliatelle (fresh, if available)

If using feathered game, roast the bird; when it is cool, pull the meat off the bone and shred it by hand. Other game should be shredded raw.

Heat olive oil in a large pot and sauté odori over medium heat. When it is full of color, add the shredded meats. Add bay leaves and thyme and continue to cook over medium heat until the meat turns a very light color. Add a good amount of wine—enough almost to cover the meat. Raise the heat and cook for 10 or 15 minutes, and enjoy the festival of smells. Add tomatoes and simmer, partially covered, over very low heat for 2 to 2½ hours, stirring often to keep the sauce from sticking to the pan, and adding water if it gets too dry.

When the sauce is almost done, add the olives. They should not cook in the sauce for longer than 5 minutes, or they will impart too strong a taste. The consistency of the sauce is important; it should be thick but not dry. If sauce becomes too dry, add a little bit of water mixed with wine or a little bit more of tomatoes, whichever you feel is lacking. Correct the sauce to your own taste.

Cook the tagliatelle in boiling water until al dente, and drain well. Add to the pan with the sauce and mix until heated over low heat.

TAGLIATELLE CON PORCINI MANTECATI

FRESH EGG NOODLES WITH PORCINI AND BUTTER

PANTRY	COLD STORAGE	MARKET
Olive oil	Garlic, smashed	Fresh porcini mushrooms, cleaned and sliced
Salt	Butter	
Black pepper	Parmesan cheese, grated	Tagliatelle (fresh, if available)

Heat olive oil in a pan and sauté garlic over medium heat until full of color. Add porcini and continue to cook over medium heat just long enough for the mushrooms to absorb the taste of garlic and oil and to release excess water. Pour off excess liquid and remove garlic. Season porcini with salt and pepper, then take them out of the pan and set aside.

Cook the tagliatelle in boiling water until al dente and drain it. Melt butter in pan, add the porcini, the cooked tagliatelle, and the Parmesan cheese. Mix thoroughly and serve.

PENNE CON SALSA ROSSA AL FUNGHETTO

QUILL-SHAPED PASTA WITH RED MUSHROOM SAUCE

PANTRY	COLD STORAGE	MARKET
Olive oil	Garlic, smashed	Fresh basil, chopped
Canned tomatoes, smashed in their own juice	Parmesan cheese	
	Salsa al Funghetto (below)	
Penne		

Heat the olive oil in a pan and sauté garlic over medium heat until golden. Remove garlic and stir in Salsa al Funghetto, tomatoes, and basil. Turn the heat to high and cook until the sauce is reduced somewhat.

Meanwhile, cook the pasta in boiling water until al dente, drain, and add to the sauce. Mix over low heat. Add Parmesan, stir again, and serve with additional Parmesan on the side.

SALSA AL FUNGHETTO

MUSHROOM SAUCE

Salsa al Funghetto is a pâté of cooked mushrooms. Keep several containers of it in the freezer to use in many Tuscan dishes. You can add a scoop of Salsa al Funghetto to stews, soups, or pastas to give the flavor of mushrooms. It will also thicken the sauce. Salsa al Funghetto can be spooned onto Fettunta (page 43) or fresh bread as an appetizer. It is the main ingredient in Salsa Rossa al Funghetto and Salsa al Funghetto in Bianco. It's also used in Penne ai Funghi e Salsiccia (page 100).

Salsa al Funghetto could be called the "sauce for all seasons" because it can be made with any mushrooms you find in the market at any time of the year. You can even make it with mushrooms not at their peak anymore— ones that are still good, but without many hours of life left. During porcini season, you can make this sauce from the stems that are left over when you grill the caps. If you freeze Salsa al Funghetto, you can have the taste of porcini all year long. Most of the time, you'll be making it with cultivated, or button, mushrooms, but the taste of the mixture can be sharpened by adding a few porcini stems, either fresh or dried.

PANTRY	COLD STORAGE	MARKET
Olive oil	Garlic, smashed	Fresh mushrooms
Salt		
Black pepper		

Mince the mushrooms until they are almost a paste. Sauté the garlic over medium heat in olive oil until full of color. Remove garlic and add mushrooms. Cook slowly until they turn a very dark brown color, almost black, and they lose most of their liquid—perhaps 15 minutes. Remove mushrooms with a slotted spoon and press out as much of the remaining liquid as possible. Discard the liquid. Season the mushrooms with salt and pepper. The sauce is the consistency of a thick puree. If used within a few days, Salsa al Funghetto can be stored in the refrigerator. If you want to keep it longer, it can be frozen for up to a month.

PENNE CON SALSA AL FUNGHETTO IN BIANCO
QUILL-SHAPED PASTA IN WHITE MUSHROOM SAUCE

PANTRY	COLD STORAGE	MARKET
Penne	Butter	Heavy cream
	Parmesan cheese, grated	
	Salsa al Funghetto (above)	

Melt the butter in a pan. Stir in Salsa al Funghetto and just enough cream so mixture is like a thick sauce. Cook the pasta in boiling water until al dente, drain well, and add to the pan with the sauce. Mix pasta as it warms over very low heat. Stir in the Parmesan and serve with additional Parmesan on the side.

PENNE AI FUNGHI E SALSICCIA

QUILL-SHAPED PASTA BAKED WITH MUSHROOM SAUCE AND SAUSAGE

PANTRY	COLD STORAGE	MARKET
Penne	Butter	Sweet and hot Italian sausages
Salt	Parmesan cheese, grated	
Black pepper	Egg whites	
	Salsa al Funghetto (page 98)	

Preheat oven to hot. Peel casing from each sausage and cook the meat over medium-low heat until thoroughly done. As it cooks, meat will break apart; if it doesn't, help it with a fork. Drain off excess fat when finished.

Meanwhile, cook the penne in boiling water until al dente and drain it. Rub butter on the inside of a baking dish and sprinkle the bottom of the dish with Parmesan. Add a layer of cooked penne, then a layer of Salsa al Funghetto, then a layer of sausage. Add salt and pepper to taste. Bury small pieces of butter everywhere in the mixture. Top with a generous sprinkling of Parmesan.

Whip the egg whites until frothy and brush over top of the dish. Bake in a hot oven until a crust is formed and top is nicely browned.

PENNE ALLA SALVIA

QUILL-SHAPED PASTA WITH SAGE AND VEAL

PANTRY	COLD STORAGE	MARKET
Olive oil	Red onion, finely chopped	Ground veal
White wine	Carrot, finely chopped	Prosciutto, chopped
Salt	Fresh parsley, finely chopped	Fresh sage
Black pepper	Beef broth	
Penne	Parmesan cheese, grated	

Heat the olive oil in a pan and brown the veal. Add the prosciutto, onion, carrot, and parsley. Stir in the sage and cover with wine; turn up the heat and cook until the wine evaporates. Stir in just enough broth to keep the mixture from sticking to the pan. Lower the heat and simmer, partially covered, for about 45 minutes. Add more broth as needed; the mixture should be moist but not runny. Season with salt and pepper.

Meanwhile, cook the pasta in boiling water until al dente, drain, and add to the pan with the sauce. Add Parmesan, mix thoroughly, and serve with additional Parmesan on the side.

FARFALLE ALLA CAPRESE

BOWTIE PASTA WITH TOMATOES, MOZZARELLA, AND BASIL

PANTRY	COLD STORAGE	MARKET
Olive oil (good-quality)		Fresh or buffalo mozzarella
Farfalle		Fresh tomatoes, chopped
Black pepper (optional)		Fresh basil

Cut the mozzarella into small cubes. Mix the tomatoes and basil together. Set aside.

Cook the pasta in boiling water until al dente, drain well, and put each portion on a warmed plate. Place the mozzarella in the center of each serving of pasta and put the tomato-basil mixture around the edge. Sprinkle with olive oil and serve. Another very good and welcome addition to this dish is black pepper.

FARFALLE CON PUMATE

BOWTIE PASTA WITH SUN-DRIED TOMATOES

This is a tomato sauce accented with the strong, sharp taste of sun-dried tomatoes. It can be used with many kinds of pasta—farfalle (which is my favorite), spaghetti, or rotelle, for example. Use an excellent quality of sun-dried tomatoes, preserved in olive oil with bay leaves. The best sun-dried tomatoes are from Liguria. I don't use any other type, unless I make them myself. I find them too sharp, too acidic, or too sour. The Ligurian tomatoes are smooth, tender, and juicy.

PANTRY	COLD STORAGE	MARKET
Olive oil	Parmesan cheese, grated	Sun-dried tomatoes
Canned tomatoes, smashed in their own juice	Fresh parsley, chopped	
Farfalle		
Black or cayenne pepper (optional)		

Cut the sun-dried tomatoes into very thin slices. Put just enough olive oil in a pan to coat the bottom, and add the sun-dried tomatoes and the canned tomatoes. Cook over medium heat until the liquid evaporates a bit.

Meanwhile, cook the pasta in boiling water until al dente, drain well, and add the pasta to the pan, mixing and cooking for a minute so the pasta can absorb the taste of the sauce. If you like a spicy taste, add pepper, but go easy because it can take away from the sharp taste of the sun-dried tomatoes.

Sprinkle with Parmesan cheese and a little parsley, and serve right away.

PENNE ALLA ROZZA

QUILL-SHAPED PASTA WITH
RUDE SAUCE

I n this recipe, rude *refers to the rough and uneven combination of the vegetables and meat. Even though the ingredients seem to be combined casually, the dish is a result of confidence in the final outcome.*

PANTRY	COLD STORAGE	MARKET
Dried porcini	Celery, chopped	Prosciutto, fairly thick, in strips
Olive oil	Red onion, thinly sliced	
Bay leaf, chopped almost to a powder	Parmesan cheese, grated	
Red wine	Butter	
Canned tomatoes, smashed in their own juice		
Penne		
Black pepper		

Soak porcini in warm water for at least 30 minutes, then drain, squeeze dry, and chop. Set aside.

Heat olive oil in a pan and add prosciutto, celery, and onion. Cook over very low heat and when the vegetables begin to soften, add the porcini and continue to cook. When the mixture begins to smell like something very good is going on, it's time to add the bay leaf and a generous amount of wine. Then add the tomatoes. Cook over high heat for a few minutes to give the flavors a chance to combine, then lower the heat and cook slowly, partially covered, for about 30 minutes.

Meanwhile, cook the penne in boiling water until al dente, drain, and stir it into the sauce along with Parmesan and a tiny bit of butter. If you see that the sauce is too dry, add a little more butter and mix. When you serve the pasta, grind some black pepper over the top, but do not cook the pepper in the sauce because it makes the prosciutto acidic and changes the taste of the dish.

PENNE AL SUGO DI PORCINI

QUILL-SHAPED PASTA WITH RED PORCINI SAUCE

PANTRY	COLD STORAGE	MARKET
Olive oil	Garlic, smashed	Fresh porcini mushrooms, sliced
Canned tomatoes, smashed in their own juice	Parmesan cheese, grated	
Anchovies (optional)		
Salt		
Black pepper		
Penne		

Heat the olive oil in a pan and sauté garlic over medium heat until golden. Remove. Add porcini and cook over high heat until they give up their liquid. Add tomatoes and cook over high heat to combine the flavors. (If you want to sharpen the taste of the sauce, add 1 or 2 anchovies with the tomatoes.) Reduce the heat and cook the sauce until it thickens. Season with salt and pepper.

Meanwhile, cook the pasta in boiling water until al dente, drain, and add it to the sauce. Mix well, add Parmesan cheese, mix some more, and serve with additional Parmesan on the side.

SPAGHETTI ALLA RUSTICA

RUSTIC-STYLE SPAGHETTI

PANTRY	COLD STORAGE	MARKET
Olive oil	Butter	
Canned tomatoes, smashed in their own juice	Red onion, thinly sliced	
Spaghetti	Parmesan cheese, grated	

Heat a mixture of olive oil and butter in a pan and sauté the onion over medium-low heat. Once you know from the smell and the color that the onion is ready—not brown, but soft and golden—add the tomatoes. Let the mixture cook slowly, uncovered, until the liquid is gone.

Meanwhile, cook the pasta in boiling water until al dente and drain it. When the sauce is ready, add a little more butter to make it more homogenous. Add the pasta to the pan, mix in Parmesan, and serve.

SPAGHETTI AL FILETTO DI POMODORO

SPAGHETTI WITH FRESH TOMATO SAUCE

For a pasta dish with fresh tomatoes you want to create a balance between delicacy and moisture. This Filetto di Pomodoro has just the right taste. One condition—the tomatoes must be extremely fresh and right.

PANTRY	COLD STORAGE	MARKET
Spaghetti	Garlic, smashed	Fresh tomatoes
Olive oil		Fresh basil, chopped (optional)

Cook the pasta in boiling water. Drain. Blanch the tomatoes by dipping them in boiling water for about a minute. Then peel them, cut them in half, squeeze out the seeds, and chop the flesh. Heat a little olive oil in a pan and sauté the garlic over medium heat. Once the garlic is browned, remove it. Add the tomatoes and let them sit in the oil for just a minute. Add the basil, if you are using it, then add the drained pasta. Toss and serve. (Don't put Parmesan cheese on this.)

SPAGHETTI ALLA PIRATA
SPAGHETTI, PIRATE STYLE

PANTRY	COLD STORAGE	MARKET
Olive oil	Garlic, smashed	Shrimp
Crushed red pepper		Mussels
White wine (good-quality)		Any available medium-size clams
Canned tomatoes, smashed in their own juice		Squid
Spaghetti		

Clean the shrimp, mussels, and clams and take them out of their shells. If the shrimp are large, chop them. Slice the squid into rings.

Heat olive oil in a large pan and sauté the garlic over medium heat until it is golden. Take it out and add the seafood. Cook over high heat for about 5 minutes, until the taste of the olive oil and garlic has been absorbed. Add red pepper to taste and pour in 2 glasses of wine. Let the wine reduce, then add enough tomatoes to cover the seafood. Still over high heat, bring the sauce to a boil, then turn the heat down to medium-low and reduce the sauce to half its quantity. This will take about 30 to 45 minutes. If sauce gets too dry, add a little bit of cold water.

Meanwhile, cook the pasta in boiling water until al dente, drain it, and add to the pan. Mix together and serve.

RIGATONI ALLA BUTTERA

PEASANT-STYLE PASTA

You can use hard-wheat pasta or fresh for this. For hard-wheat pasta, I suggest rigatoni or penne; for fresh, I suggest tagliatelle or pappardelle. Definitely never use spaghetti.

PANTRY	COLD STORAGE	MARKET
Black pepper	Butter	Sweet and hot Italian sausages
Canned tomatoes, smashed in their own juice	Parmesan cheese, grated	Green peas, parboiled
Hard-wheat pasta (optional)		Heavy cream
		Fresh pasta (optional)

Peel the casings off the sausages and break the meat into chunks. Cook over medium-low heat in a pan without oil; the natural fat in the sausages renders enough grease to keep them from sticking. The sausages will crumble even more once the fat is released. When meat is cooked through, drain the sausages of excess fat, add some pepper, and set aside.

In a large pan, melt a generous spoonful of butter and add the cooked sausage, the peas, and the tomatoes. Mix well and turn up the heat. Cook until the sauce thickens and the peas are tender. Add cream and reduce further. Add enough Parmesan cheese to thicken the sauce; it should be very thick, uniform, and moist.

Meanwhile, cook the pasta in boiling water until al dente, drain, and add to the pan with the sauce. Add more Parmesan, mix thoroughly over low heat, and serve with additional Parmesan cheese on the side.

MAREMMA

*M*aremma *is the most harmonious area of Tuscany. There are mountains, beaches, hills, and fields—anything you could ever want. Even though Maremma was once* acquitrino, *a land of marsh and quicksand, today it is a wild, earthy, fertile, rich province.*

The farmhouses of Maremma are always in the middle of nowhere, with white stucco walls, green windows, and red roofs. In front of every Tuscan house in the country is a yard with a tree, and attached to the tree is a dog— always a dog. This area is the aia. *There is no explanation of the origin of this word. It's a real Tuscan word, with a beautiful sound, and it is the name for that open space where the pigs, chickens, rabbits, cows, lambs, goats, and ducks are kept. We cook them all, and they're all good.*

In the summertime I remember going to my grandmother's house on the coast in Maremma. When the sun is hot and beats down and you feel it on your head, it's nice to be near the sea. I remember days when it was very hot and dry—nothing moved—and then suddenly a wind started to slowly grow and grow. It was the Tra-montana that comes at sunset— the wind of purification before the night came. Suddenly you feel it and it brings every smell you love: the sharp smell of the sea mixed with the grass of the fields.

People in Maremma have a hard and deep way of looking at you when they don't know you, but then they come out with a very beautiful smile that lets you know there's really a warm person behind there.

In Maremma, the hospitality is the kind that when your friends say, "Stop by and see me," they mean you have to stay for one whole meal or at least a snack. You've got to eat. Not eating something is out of the question.

In Maremma, people are always kissing and hugging, yelling and screaming at each other. That's just the way they are. You could be standing right next to them and they scream, "HOW ARE YOU?" They talk so loud they could break your eardrum. You're always having to tell them, "I'm right here, not out in the ocean."

They remind me of Texans. The first time I heard a man from Texas, I thought, "My God, I feel like I'm in Maremma again."

SPAGHETTI ALLA MAREMMANA

SPAGHETTI, MAREMMA STYLE

This is a dish special to the Maremma region of Tuscany. Within this area, which is only a hundred kilometers long and forty wide, I've seen this dish made in five or six different versions because of the imaginative way the people cook. Any recipe with "Maremma" in the name has a very strong, sharp taste. This recipe is made with few ingredients, but all of them have strong flavors. I love to use spaghetti for this dish, but you can use penne as well. Pecorino cheese is better than Parmesan here because it's sharper. The dish can be made in any season. In the summertime, use really fresh, ripe tomatoes, which you just chop up and throw in, let cook, and mix.

PANTRY	COLD STORAGE	MARKET
Olive oil	Garlic, smashed	Fresh mushrooms, any variety, chunked
Salt		Eggplant, peeled and chopped into chunks the same size as mushrooms
Black pepper		
Red wine		Green peas
Canned tomatoes, smashed in their own juice (or fresh, in season)		Sweet Italian sausage
		Caciotta or pecorino cheese, grated

Heat the olive oil in a pan and sauté the garlic over medium heat until full of color. Remove garlic and add mushrooms, eggplant, and peas. Peel the casing off the sausage and break up the meat with your hand. Add it to the pan and continue to cook over medium heat until the ingredients combine and begin to color. Add salt and pepper to taste. Stir constantly so the mixture doesn't stick to the bottom of the pan. Turn the heat up to high, cover the mixture with red wine, mix some more, and continue to cook. Enjoy the beautiful, strong smell of the sauce and the vegetables. When your nose tells you, "This is good; let's keep it like this," add the tomatoes and turn the heat down a little bit. Let the mixture cook for 20 minutes and if the sauce gets too dry, add more red wine—just a small amount.

Meanwhile, cook the pasta in boiling water until it is al dente and drain it. Add it to the pan with the sauce, add the cheese, and mix thoroughly over low heat. Serve with additional grated cheese on the side.

SPAGHETTI ALLE VONGOLE IN BIANCO
SPAGHETTI IN WHITE CLAM SAUCE

PANTRY	COLD STORAGE	MARKET
Olive oil	Garlic, sliced	Cherrystone, Littleneck, or Manilla clams in the shell
Crushed red pepper	Fresh parsley, chopped	
Spaghetti		

Let the clams sit in water to cover for at least an hour and then wash them very well.

Pour enough olive oil in a deep pan to cover the bottom. Add garlic and red pepper and turn up the heat. When the oil is very, very hot, stand back and add the clams. Cover and let them steam until the shells are completely opened. Discard any clams that remain shut.

Meanwhile, cook the pasta in boiling, salted water and drain. At this point you have 2 choices. You can simply leave the clams in the shells, add the pasta, toss, and serve. Or, you can remove the clams from their shells, discard the shells, and return the clams to the pan with the water from the clams, olive oil, and garlic. Turn up the heat for a few minutes to reduce the liquid, add the cooked pasta, toss, and serve. If you do it the second way, the pasta absorbs the juice and clam taste right away and it is much more flavorful than if simply tossed with the clams in their shells.

SPAGHETTINI AL CACIO E PEPE
SPAGHETTINI WITH GOAT CHEESE AND PEPPER

PANTRY	COLD STORAGE	MARKET
Olive oil		Aged, sharp goat cheese or sheep's milk cheese, shredded
Black pepper		
Spaghettini		

Heat some olive oil in a pan with lots of freshly ground black pepper. Cook the pasta in boiling water until al dente, then drain. Put the cheese into the pan, then add the pasta. Toss quickly and serve with a drop or two of olive oil on top. This is a slightly dry, sharp-tasting dish.

SPAGHETTI CON AGLIO, OLIO, E PEPERONCINO
SPAGHETTI WITH GARLIC, OLIVE OIL, AND HOT PEPPER

*E*veryone knows about this very simple recipe, but not everyone knows the secret of its greatness: the garlic cooked until golden in the olive oil, the taste of the hot pepper, and the timing. The pasta must be ready, al dente, to be added hot to the sauce. Make sure that the sauce doesn't come out too liquid or too dry.

PANTRY	COLD STORAGE	MARKET
Olive oil	Garlic, thinly sliced	Fresh, whole hot peppers (optional)
Crushed red pepper (optional)		
Spaghetti		

Generously cover the bottom of a pan with olive oil and place over low heat. Add a whole fresh pepper or a pinch of crushed red pepper and the garlic. Sauté until garlic is golden. If you have used fresh pepper, remove it. Add cooked, drained spaghetti to the pan, mix well, and serve in a very hot dish. Taste for spiciness. If the dish isn't fiery enough, add more pepper. The spaghetti should be ready when the garlic turns golden, so nothing gets cold. Timing is essential here because the sauce cannot be set aside.

The only thing you can add to this dish is nothing. Especially not cheese. I know many people like cheese on pasta, but it's unnecessary here.

NOTE Here's another way to make the dish, which will make the sauce spicier. Add the fresh pepper to the water in which the pasta is cooking. Use 2 or 3 peppers for a gallon of water.

SPAGHETTI CON BROCCOLETTI E RADICCHIO

SPAGHETTI WITH BROCCOLI RABE AND RADICCHIO

If you can grow broccoli, then you can grow broccoli rabe. It's strange, but in many parts of this country there is just the right environment to grow broccoli rabe, but usually you only find it where there is a big Italian population. Anyway, here's a dish for all the Italians in the United States.

PANTRY	COLD STORAGE	MARKET
Olive oil	Garlic, thinly sliced	Broccoli rabe
Salt		Radicchio
Black pepper		
Crushed red pepper		
Spaghetti		

Preheat oven to hot. Cut the stems off the broccoli rabe and throw them away. Soak the flowers and leaves in water for a few minutes so all the dirt is removed. Cut the head of radicchio in half and then into tiny pieces, then bake the pieces with a bit of olive oil, salt, and pepper until crisp and crunchy. Set aside.

In a deep pan, sauté a generous amount of red pepper and garlic in olive oil over medium heat. When the oil is very hot—just smoking—add the broccoli rabe and the radicchio, but keep your face away—the oil will jump. Mix the radicchio and broccoli rabe and then cover the pan for about a minute until they wilt.

Cook the spaghetti in boiling water until al dente, then drain, but save a few drops of cooking water and add it to the pan with the broccoli rabe and radicchio. Mix the pasta and vegetables well, toss with more olive oil, and continue to cook for a minute or so. Serve on a warmed plate, topped with a little more olive oil. Don't put on any cheese; it's not necessary because the cheese will soften the particular taste of the broccoli rabe.

SPAGHETTI AL SUGO DI SPIGOLA

SPAGHETTI WITH SEA BASS SAUCE

*O*f course, you can use any type of white fish that you like. I've made this dish using striped bass, red snapper, and grouper. The sauce is based on the concept of the meat sauce Bolognese, but uses fish instead. Once the fish is ground up and cooked for about an hour and a half, what remains is the essence of the fish and the fragrance of onions, garlic, and wine.

PANTRY	COLD STORAGE	MARKET
Olive oil		Sea bass or other white fish
White wine (good-quality)		Oregano, thyme, or rosemary (fresh, if available), chopped
Canned tomatoes, smashed in their own juice		
Crushed red pepper (optional)		
Spaghetti		
Black pepper		
Odori (page 30)		

Have the fish cleaned, boned, and skinned at the market. Cut the flesh into pieces and set aside. Cook the odori in olive oil over medium heat until soft. If you are using fresh herbs, add them now; otherwise, add them at the end of the recipe. Add the fish and continue to cook over medium heat until it loses its water. Add enough wine to cover and reduce the liquid over high heat. Remove the fish from the liquid, grind it up, and return puree to the pot. Cover with the tomatoes, bring to a boil, and then turn the heat to low. Let the mixture cook, partially covered, for 1½ to 2 hours. (If you like spicy sauces, add red pepper at the same time you add the tomatoes.) Don't let the sauce dry out completely; add water if necessary to keep it moist.

Meanwhile, cook the spaghetti in boiling water until it is al dente and drain it. (If you are using dried herbs, add them now to the sauce.) Then add the spaghetti to the pot, stir to mix, grind some black pepper on top, drizzle with a bit of olive oil, and serve.

THE FLOOD OF 1966

When my mother told me about Tuscany during World War II, I found her description of the misery and poverty unbelievable. The simplest provisions, like milk and bread, were impossible to find. I was a kid when she told me these stories, and I thought she was exaggerating just to scare me so I would understand how our life wasn't always as easy as I had known it.

Then in 1966 there was a huge flood in Tuscany. The night before I had come home for the holidays from my boarding school near Genoa. The river Arno and many other rivers in Tuscany came over their banks, and almost everything—honestly—was covered with water. It was like a huge rug rolling out over the land covering everything in its path: cars, houses, animals. It was the most apocalyptic sight I've ever seen. In the old part of Florence the water was twenty-five feet above street level. The most valuable buildings in the city were underwater. The damage was unbelievable.

There I was, stuck in the house for almost ten days with no way to get back to school. The first day I didn't think much about it, but by the second day I started to realize that certain provisions were missing. There was no fresh food, no milk, no coffee. You can deal with that kind of adversity for one or two days, then you want to eat. We had almost nothing left, because we had already gone through one lunch, one dinner, and one breakfast. Remember, in Tuscany we do our shopping at the markets every day.

Eventually the only things left in the house were two huge containers of ricotta. My mother boiled some penne, then, in the bottom of a large bowl, she put some of the hot water from the pasta pot and added some ricotta, a little sugar and cinnamon, and the penne. I thought, "What the hell is this?" It was an excellent dish of pasta, full of taste. It made you feel better as long as you weren't looking out the window at the water still rising.

We had this pasta for one dinner and one lunch, then we got some canned food from the military forces. But this is a dish that belongs in the records of human survival. In any catastrophe, there seems to be one dish that pulls you through, and this was ours.

ROTELLE CON RICOTTA E CANNELLA

PINWHEEL PASTA WITH RICOTTA AND CINNAMON

*N*utmeg is something we use a lot of in Tuscany, and I always use nutmeg with ricotta cheese. Nutmeg has a subtle flavor that's there but not there—nobody seems to know what it is. I'm crazy about the dishes I do with nutmeg. In America people eat a lot of cinnamon. Cinnamon is complementary to nutmeg, but nutmeg is sharper. Children love this dish for lunch because of its mild, sweet taste.

PANTRY	COLD STORAGE	MARKET
Rotelle or penne		**Ricotta cheese**
Nutmeg or cinnamon		
Sugar (optional)		

Put the rotelle on to boil and, while it is cooking, place a pan or bowl near the burner, but not directly over the heat. Put as much ricotta as you think you need into the warm bowl or pan, depending on how much you like the taste. Sprinkle the ricotta with a bit of cinnamon or nutmeg, again to your taste. If you want to sweeten the dish, add very little sugar. I personally suggest a little sugar.

Once the rotelle is cooked al dente, drain it, but save a few tablespoons of the pasta water. Add this with the rotelle to the warm ricotta and mix well. The hot pasta will warm the ricotta. Serve at once.

ROTELLE AL POMODORO E PARMIGIANO

PINWHEEL PASTA WITH TOMATO SAUCE AND PARMESAN CHEESE

PANTRY	COLD STORAGE	MARKET
Rotelle	Parmesan cheese, grated	Tomatoes (fresh, if available)
		Heavy cream

If you are using canned tomatoes, smash them in their own juice; if you are using fresh tomatoes, make them into a Filetto di Pomodoro (page 105). Sauté the tomatoes over medium heat with a touch of cream to make a very light and creamy pink sauce. Cook the pasta until al dente, drain, and add to the sauce with a very little Parmesan cheese. Serve.

FRITTATA DI PASTA

ITALIAN OMELETTE WITH PASTA

In 1968, the students in my school went on strike. One morning at the opening of classes, we kicked out all the teachers and occupied the classrooms. It was a scary situation because the police had surrounded the school, and we knew they were going to break in. By early afternoon tensions were high and we were preparing for a confrontation when, all of a sudden, someone at the window yelled to me, "Pino, it's your mother." I thought, "Damn it, she's always underfoot when I don't need her." There she was, standing in a crowd of policemen, holding a big picnic basket. They wouldn't let her give it to me until they checked it for arms. Although they didn't find guns, what they did find was my lunch in the form of Frittata di Pasta, fresh bread, a bottle of wine, napkins, silverware, and salt and pepper. She must have thought we were having a picnic in there. I was very embarrassed because I was already known as the student whose mother packed his book bag with richly stuffed panini *every day.*

The only place she didn't follow me was to jail that night. She tried, but they wouldn't let her in.

PANTRY	COLD STORAGE	MARKET
Olive oil	Eggs, beaten	
Leftover pasta in its sauce		
Salt		
Black pepper		

Put a little olive oil in a pan set over medium heat and add all the pasta. Then put the eggs on top and let them seep down. Add salt and pepper, and when the frittata is brown on one side, turn it over and let it get brown on the other side. It comes out very crunchy.

I RISOTTI

ROMANCING
THE
RISOTTO

When you make a risotto you should be in perfect harmony with yourself. You shouldn't be nervous or angry. It's a ritual that is going to give you so much pleasure later that it's worth spending fifteen or twenty minutes over a hot stove stirring very slowly. It can be like seducing a woman. She doesn't know you, and you need to work things out with her slowly—meeting, flirting, getting to know each other, and wanting each other. That's what a good risotto is all about. It's the dish of romance. If you rush it's never good.

The basic technique is this: heat the butter or oil in a heavy pan and sauté the vegetables, onions, garlic, or whatever else the recipe calls for. When the vegetables are soft but not brown, add the rice, one generous fistful per person. Stir continually to coat the rice with oil or butter. Have twice as much broth as the amount of rice you plan to use. If you run out of broth, you can use water. Add a ladleful of broth to the rice and continue stirring. When all the liquid has been absorbed, add more broth. Only add more liquid when the rice has absorbed what is in the pan. Never add too much at one time—the rice should never look soaked. It should be halfway between wet and dry, but never soupy; otherwise, the rice boils and it won't absorb the taste of the other ingredients. Continue this process for fifteen or twenty minutes, stirring continually and adding liquid as it is absorbed. Adjust the heat as you cook. It should be low enough so that nothing sticks to the bottom of the pan, but high enough so that everything is bubbling in a lively way. The risotto is done when the center of the rice is slightly firm and not bright white. As with pasta, taste a kernel to see if it's done. The customary way to eat risotto is to flatten it on the plate with your fork so that it will cool evenly, and then begin eating it from the outside edge.

Preceding page: **Arborio rice**

RISOTTO AI FUNGHI FRESCHI

RISOTTO WITH FRESH MUSHROOMS

PANTRY	COLD STORAGE	MARKET
Olive oil	Garlic, smashed	Fresh mushrooms: chanterelles, shiitakes, golden oaks, cremini, or whatever else is available
Salt	Chicken or vegetable broth	
Black pepper	Butter	
Arborio rice	Parmesan cheese, grated	

Clean the mushrooms and separate the hats from the stems. Slice the hats, chop the stems, and set aside.

Heat olive oil in a pan and sauté a clove of garlic over medium heat until golden. Remove garlic, then add the sliced mushroom hats and sauté them over high heat. When they are cooked, season with salt and pepper and set aside in a bowl with their juice.

Add a bit more olive oil to the pan and sauté another clove of garlic over medium heat until it is full of color. Remove it, then add the mushroom stems and sauté them over high heat. Add the rice and broth and reduce heat. Continue cooking the risotto as described on the preceding page.

When the risotto is almost done and almost dry, stir in the reserved caps and mushroom liquid; this is the last liquid you will add. Continue stirring until the mushroom liquid is absorbed. Add some butter to hold the risotto together and make it richer. Sprinkle with Parmesan and serve.

RISOTTO CON SPINACI

RISOTTO WITH SPINACH

T his dish is also called *Risotto alla Fiorentina* because Florentines eat a lot of spinach. Spinach is available throughout the year, so this is a risotto for all seasons.

PANTRY	COLD STORAGE	MARKET
Olive oil	Red onion, chopped	Spinach, stems removed and leaves chopped
Arborio rice	Chicken or vegetable broth	
Salt		Fresh mint, chopped
Black pepper	Butter	Fresh basil, chopped
	Parmesan cheese, grated	

Heat the olive oil in a heavy pan and sauté the onion over medium heat until golden. Add the spinach and sauté until it wilts. Add the mint and basil to the spinach. Stir, then lower the heat, add the rice and broth, and continue cooking the risotto as described on page 120. When the rice has reached the desired consistency, add enough butter to hold it together and enrich the taste. Season with salt and pepper and mix in the Parmesan cheese.

RISOTTO CON PISELLI VERDI

RISOTTO WITH GREEN PEAS

PANTRY	COLD STORAGE	MARKET
Olive oil	Red onions, minced	Green peas, fresh or frozen
Arborio rice	Garlic, smashed	
Salt	Chicken or vegetable broth	
Black pepper	Butter	
	Parmesan cheese, grated	

Steam or boil the peas until they are half cooked. Mash about one third of the peas and add the onions to this puree. Set aside. Leave the remaining peas whole.

Heat olive oil in a pan and sauté garlic until golden. Remove the garlic, add the whole peas, and stir until well coated with oil. Lower the heat, add the rice and broth, and continue cooking the risotto as described on page 120.

When the risotto has been cooking for 5 or 10 minutes, add the pea-onion mixture and continue cooking until the rice is done. Stir in enough butter to hold it together and enrich the taste. Season with salt and pepper and sprinkle with Parmesan.

RISOTTO ALLA CONTADINA
PEASANT-STYLE RISOTTO

*T*his dish is excellent on a cold winter night, served with raw scallions dipped in olive oil to which black pepper has been added and with a rich, heavy red wine.

PANTRY	COLD STORAGE	MARKET
Olive oil	Red onion, finely chopped	Peas (fresh if available, or frozen)
Arborio rice	Chicken or vegetable broth	Hot and sweet sausage in equal amounts, peeled
Salt	Butter	
Black pepper	Parmesan cheese, grated	

If using fresh peas, boil until barely tender; if using frozen, allow them to defrost and come to room temperature.

Heat oil in a heavy pan and sauté the onion over medium heat until golden. Add the sausage and cook over high heat, breaking up meat as it cooks. When the sausage has changed color but is still moist, add the rice and broth, lower the heat, and continue to cook the risotto as described on page 120. When the rice has reached the desired consistency, add the peas and enough butter to hold the mixture together and enrich the taste. Season with salt and pepper and mix in the Parmesan cheese. Serve hot.

RISOTTO AL POMODORO E BASILICO

RISOTTO WITH TOMATOES AND BASIL

This dish is pleasing in any season. In winter use good-quality imported canned tomatoes. In the summer use the ripest fresh plum or cherry tomatoes available.

PANTRY	COLD STORAGE	MARKET
Olive oil	Chicken or vegetable broth	Tomatoes (fresh, if available)
Arborio rice	Garlic, whole cloves	Fresh basil, half chopped and half left whole
Salt	Parmesan cheese, grated (optional)	

If you are using fresh tomatoes, blanch them in boiling water, peel them, mash them in a bowl, then dilute them with enough broth to make them juicy. If you are using canned tomatoes, omit the broth and mash them in their own juice.

Heat oil in a heavy pan and sauté the garlic over medium heat until golden. Remove the garlic and add enough tomatoes to cover the bottom of the pan by about 1 inch. Lower the heat, add the rice, and continue to cook the risotto as described on page 120, adding the chopped basil. When the rice has reached the desired consistency, add the whole basil leaves, season with salt and pepper, and mix in the optional Parmesan cheese. Serve hot.

RISOTTO ALLE VONGOLE IN BIANCO

RISOTTO IN WHITE CLAM SAUCE

This is the most delicate way to prepare clams. Clams are wonderful with pasta, of course, but here the rice adds a smoothness to the seafood that gives it a different taste.

PANTRY	COLD STORAGE	MARKET
Olive oil	Garlic, whole cloves	Cherrystone, Littleneck, or Manilla clams, cleaned, removed from shells, and reserved in their own water
Arborio rice	Butter	
Salt	Fresh parsley, finely chopped	
Crushed red pepper	Fish broth (optional)	
White wine (optional)		

If needed, add enough fish broth and white wine to the clams to be sure you have enough liquid to make the risotto. Set aside.

Heat the oil in a heavy pan and sauté the garlic over medium heat until golden. Remove the garlic and add enough clams with clam water to cover the bottom of the pan by about 1 inch. Lower the heat, add the rice, and continue cooking the risotto as described on page 120, adding additional clams and clam water and broth or white wine as needed. When the rice has reached the desired consistency, add any clams you have left over (without broth) and enough butter to bind the mixture together. Season with salt (if needed; the clam broth is salty) and the crushed red pepper. Add the parsley, mix well, and serve hot.

RISOTTO ALLA PESCATORA

RISOTTO, FISHERMAN'S STYLE

PANTRY	COLD STORAGE	MARKET
Olive oil	Red onions, finely chopped	Cherrystone, Littleneck, or Manilla clams, cleaned, removed from shells, and reserved in their own water
Arborio rice	Garlic, whole cloves	
Crushed red pepper	Butter	
Canned tomatoes	Fresh parsley, finely chopped	
Salt		Mussels, cleaned and removed from shells
White wine		Squid, cleaned, sliced into rings, and boiled until tender
		Small shrimp, shelled

Combine seafood in a bowl with the clam broth. Make sure you have enough liquid for making the risotto. Otherwise use white wine. Heat olive oil in a heavy pan and sauté the onions and garlic over medium heat until golden. Remove the garlic and add enough seafood to cover the bottom of the pan by about 2 inches. Season with the crushed red pepper and continue to cook over lowered heat, adding the rice, tomatoes, and seafood as described on page 120. When the rice has reached the desired consistency, add enough butter to hold the mixture together. Season with salt, mix in the parsley, and serve hot.

RISOTTO NERO
ALLE SEPPIE

BLACK RICE STEWED WITH
CUTTLEFISH, OR BLACK SQUID

If it should ever happen in your lifetime that you come across a cuttlefish in any fish market, buy it, because this recipe can only be made with a cuttlefish. The cuttlefish has more or less the look of a squid and lives in the Mediterranean Sea, but its peculiar quality is a special ink which is very important to the success of this dish. To prepare the cuttlefish, first separate the hat from the tentacles and remove the bones. Then turn the hat inside out. You'll recognize the stomach; this is no good, so just throw it away. Keep the tiny black bag that contains the ink. You can't miss it; it's the only black one. This container of ink is what the cuttlefish uses for self-defense in its day-to-day life.

PANTRY	COLD STORAGE	MARKET
Olive oil	Garlic, smashed	Cuttlefish
White wine	Red onions, finely chopped	
Arborio rice	Vegetable or fish broth	
Salt	Butter	
Black pepper		

Wash the hats and tentacles of the cuttlefish well and cut into chunks. Heat oil in a pan, add garlic, and sauté over medium heat until golden. Remove garlic, add onions, and sauté them until golden. Add cuttlefish, wine, and broth and cook over very low heat until soft and tender; this could take up to 1 hour. If you see that the pan is getting dry, add water.

When the cuttlefish is soft and tender and the liquid has been absorbed, add ink, rice, and broth over the heat and continue to cook the risotto as described on page 120. The bag of ink will break up as you stir, and the rice will become dark gray or black. At the end of the cooking time, add just enough butter to hold the risotto together. Season with salt and pepper to taste.

IL PESCE

GRANDPA'S NETS AND GRANDMA'S POTS

My mother's family comes from Orbetello, a village situated on a tiny tongue of land about eight miles long, which connects Monte Argentario to the coast of Maremma. Orbetello is the largest place in Tuscany for the cultivation of eels. The people who live in Orbetello are a different kind of Tuscan. They are rough and genuine, like the peasants you find inland in Maremma, but they have the sweetness of people living next to the sea.

My grandfather was a fisherman. His name was Ettore, but everyone called him "Bo," which is an exclamation in dialect that means "Beats me" or "Don't ask me" or "How should I know?" Like the rest of the family, he was anti-Fascist. During World War II, the Fascists put him in charge of all the civilians in Orbetello, and it was his responsibility to report anyone who did anything against the uniformed soldiers who occupied the town. They would say something like, "There is a man up in the hills. We are looking for him. Do you know where he is hiding?" And my grandfather would shrug his shoulders and say, "Bo?" So he was known as Bo Solimeno until the day he died.

I was only three years old when Bo first took me to the osteria, or local wine bar, where all the fishermen gathered after work to drink beer and wine and to play cards. Then we would take the fish home to my grandmother, and I would watch her make fish stew or dry the eels.

I've never seen anyone clean eels the way my grandfather did. What a guy! He would hook his thumb in the mouth of the eel, pull down, and open up the eel like a zipper, taking the interiors out as he pulled. His skin was like leather. I have tried this four or five times, and the only thing I ever got was hurt. After my grandfather cleaned the eels, my grandmother would sometimes hang the eels by clothespins on a line to dry, the same way people hang their shirts and pants. She would hang fifty or sixty of these beautiful eels in the sun. Other times, my grandfather would take a fresh eel and marinate it in a huge glass jar to make Scaveccio (page 132). He'd say, "These are stored for the best moments and the worst moments," meaning any celebration like a birthday, but also for the wintertime, when you can't go fishing and there's nothing good to eat.

My grandmother was a religious person, but my grandfather was not, so when he died there was a problem. When we arrived at the house the day after my grandfather died, we found out that my grandmother had ordered a coffin. My mother said, "Coffin? What for? He's not going to be buried in any cemetery. That's his last wish. He told me, 'I'm a fisherman. When I die, I don't want to finish in the dirt. I want to be burned—cooked and thrown into the water. That's where I belong and that's where I want to go. I can't stay in a grave; I'm claustrophobic.'" My grandmother said, "Yes, I know. I'm going to respect his last wish, but I also have to respect my feelings, so we're going to have a burial—but without him." So she had a funeral with an empty coffin, and now she has a grave in the cemetery to visit every day.

I sat with the rest of the family in the huge living room, looking at my grandfather's body, everything silent and solemn and still. Then, suddenly, I was aware of a familiar sound in the background. You could barely hear it, but from the other side of the house, dishes and silver-ware were rattling. The kitchen was working; dinner was being prepared for the wake.

I knew we were going to be there quite a few hours so something would be eaten, but I didn't expect a whole meal. I didn't think my grandmother had the strength at that time to think, "What kind of menu should we serve tonight?" But it was polenta with eel, the eel cut into chunks, stewed with tomatoes, put on top of polenta, and served as a first course. Then we had baccalà, which is dried codfish. That was always in the house because it's marinated in salt, completely dry, and keeps for months. This baccalà was first boiled for a long time to get the salt out, then dipped into egg yolk and flour and fried.

We have a custom in some parts of Tuscany that when someone dies you're not supposed to drink white wine—even with fish. Only red wine shows the proper respect at a funeral. Since most people drink white wine with fish and red wine with meat, it seems like this custom is a form of punishment people inflict on themselves in memory of the dead. I've asked many people why and nobody knows.

LO SCAVECCIO

MARINATED EEL

This dish, unique to Maremma, is one you can make in winter as well as summer. It's a very good, tasty appetizer served with a nice piece of peasant bread. It sounds so good, I wish I could have some right now. Use a medium-size eel, about one foot long. Eels are available all year in Chinese markets and at Christmas in many Italian fish markets.

PANTRY	COLD STORAGE	MARKET
Corn oil	Garlic, smashed	Eel, cleaned and cut into 2- or 3-inch pieces
Olive oil		
White wine vinegar		Fresh rosemary
Crushed red pepper		

Put a mixture of corn oil and olive oil in a frying pan and fry the eel on both sides over high heat until pimples start to show on the skin and it begins to separate from the meat. When a fork penetrates the eel very easily, take the pieces out of the pan. Let them rest on some paper towels to blot the excess oil.

Meanwhile, in a saucepan mix enough vinegar with a few branches of rosemary, a few cloves of garlic, and some red pepper—enough liquid to cover the eel. Slowly bring this mixture to a low boil, then turn off the heat. Put the eel into the liquid and let sit until cool. Then spoon eel and liquid into jars to store. Eat right away, or refrigerate. The eel will keep for a long time.

MY UNCLE'S RESERVOIR

My uncle, the fisherman, is in his late fifties, but he looks much older because his skin has been cooked by the sun for too many seasons. He took me to see a reservoir that he and the other fishermen built to catch fish. He told me, "You know, Pino, for years and years your grandfather and I and all my brothers and all the fishermen of Orbetello went out with the boats every morning until finally, we got smart. Knowing how the sea runs into the bay, we found a way not to have to go out to the fish, but to have the fish come to us." He showed me a very simple system. When the fish come in at high tide, they swim through an open gate into the reservoir. Then the gate is lowered, and when the fish want to follow the tide out, the big ones are trapped; only the smaller ones can swim to freedom. The only thing the fishermen have to do is go down to the reservoir early in the morning with the nets and pull the fish out by the ton.

I'm glad for my uncle, but I'm also sorry to see disappear the ritual of going fishing every day— but that's only my point of view. The practical view is that those men don't have to break their backs and risk their lives going out in all kinds of weather.

As my uncle and I were talking, we saw a fish leap about ten feet out of the water in an effort to find the sea, but he only landed on his face in the sand. My uncle simply picked him up, washed him off, and put him in a container of water to save him for the next day's market.

Fishermen at rest, Orbetello

ABOUT FISH

CHOOSING FISH You can tell a really fresh fish by its gills and eyes. The gills have to be red, and the eyes still have to look alive. You know how we say in Italian, "He has the look of a dead fish?" You don't want to eat a fish that looks like that —so dead looking that it's good for nothing. It may be dead, but it should still look lively.

CLEANING FISH Scale and clean the fish, or have it done at the fish market, but don't have it boned. When I talk about preparing fish, I mean the *whole* fish. Never bone a fish until after it's cooked. The skin protects the fish during cooking the same way it protected the fish when it was in the water. If the fish is filleted, it tends to get dry and tough or, if you poach it, too moist. If the fish is cooked whole, the skin acts as

protection from too much heat or moisture. Of course, it is possible to do all these recipes with filleted fish, but the dish is not going to taste the same. One reason people fillet fish is because they are scared of the bones, but don't be afraid to enjoy food. When you eat fish, your tongue and your teeth will tell you if there is something in your mouth you don't want to swallow. If there is, spit it out. Anyway, it's easy to lift out the bones with a fork after the fish is cooked. But check carefully before serving.

SUBSTITUTIONS Dentice, spigola, cefalo, sogliole, or any other kind of Mediterranean fish mentioned in these recipes can be replaced with common U.S. fish, such as red snapper, striped bass, pompano, grouper, mullet, or scrod.

INSALATA DI PESCE CON VEGETALI
COLD FISH AND VEGETABLE SALAD

*A*ny number of dishes can be made from fish combined with vegetables. Let your imagination go and choose vegetables that you feel go with the taste of fish. I once had a fish salad with fresh boiled cannellini beans. I've used green beans when they're in season—the tiny delicate ones. You can add carrots, potatoes, whatever. You don't need a heavy sauce of butter and cream; keep things light.

PANTRY	COLD STORAGE	MARKET
Olive oil	Red onion	Snapper, striped bass, grouper, or porgy
Cannellini beans (optional)	Garlic, whole cloves	
Red wine vinegar or lemon juice	Potatoes (optional)	Any seasonal vegetables: celery, green beans, carrots, asparagus, zucchini
Salt		
Black pepper		

Place the fish, onion, garlic, and celery in a deep pan and cover with water. Cook over medium heat until the fish is tender. Then slowly, with some patience, strain out the broth; discard the onion, garlic, and celery. Break up the fish and check for bones. Lightly steam or blanch the vegetables you've chosen, then combine them with the pieces of fish. Stir in oil and vinegar or lemon juice to taste and season with salt and pepper. Serve at room temperature or slightly chilled.

INSALATA DI MARE ALLA TOSCANA

COLD SEAFOOD SALAD, TUSCAN STYLE

PANTRY	COLD STORAGE	MARKET
Olive oil	Garlic, sliced	Cherrystone, Littleneck, or Manilla clams
Salt	Fresh parsley, chopped	
Black pepper	Lemon juice and wedges	Baby shrimp, out of the shell
Green or black olives		Squid

Soak the clams in cold water until they release sand. Steam the clams until they open and remove them from their shells, discarding any that haven't opened. Strain them and set aside the broth.

In 2 separate pots, steam the shrimp and the squid until they are white and tender. Mix the clams, shrimp, and squid in enough olive oil to moisten well and place them in a bowl with the sliced garlic, parsley, lemon juice, salt, and pepper. Add some reserved clam broth and serve cold with lemon wedges and olives.

SOGLIOLA ARROSTO

ROASTED SOLE

PANTRY	COLD STORAGE	MARKET
Salt		Sole: one 1-pound fish per person
Black pepper		Rosemary (fresh, if possible)
Olive oil		

Preheat the oven to hot. Clean the fish, season with salt and pepper, stuff with rosemary, and rub with a good quantity of olive oil, inside and out.

Lay the fish in a shallow pan and roast in the oven. Start to check after 6 minutes. You will know when the fish is done if you penetrate it with a fork to the spine and the fork comes out easily. Or gently push aside some of the meat, and if it is white, the fish is done.

PESCE ARROSTO CON PATATE

FISH ROASTED WITH POTATOES

The day of Ferragosto—the Feast of the Assumption—is a big holiday all over Italy, and I remember both my grandmother and my mother making this dish for lunch. This is a one-dish meal, excellent made at home. I can't do it in the restaurant because people would have to wait too long while it cooked. But it's worth waiting for at home.

PANTRY	COLD STORAGE	MARKET
Olive oil		Whole baby snapper, pompano, bass, or grouper: 1 pound of fish per person, minimum 4 pounds
Salt		
Black pepper		
		New potatoes, cut into small chunks
		Rosemary (fresh, if available)

Preheat the oven to medium-hot. Have the fish cleaned and scaled, but leave the heads on. Wet the bottom and sides of a baking dish with olive oil and place the fish in it. Put the potatoes all around the fish. Tuck sprigs of rosemary all around, then sprinkle with salt, pepper, and olive oil. Roast in the oven for about 30 minutes. Check every 10 minutes to see that potatoes don't stick to the pan. You will know when the fish is done when you penetrate it with a fork to the spine and the fork comes out easily. The potatoes should be done, too. If you are using a smaller fish, I suggest you parboil the potatoes first, so they will be done at the same time as the fish.

DENTICE AL GUAZZETTO

WHOLE BABY GROUPER OR RED SNAPPER POACHED IN TOMATO SAUCE

Guazzetto *means poached in an appetizing sauce that makes you forget about the fish once you dip bread into it. You can offer the fish whole or fillet it before serving and pour the sauce on top.*

PANTRY	COLD STORAGE	MARKET
All-purpose flour	Garlic, smashed	Grouper or red snapper: One 1-pound fish per person, left whole
Olive oil	Fish or vegetable broth	
White wine	Fresh parsley, chopped	
Salt		Tomatoes (fresh or canned; see Note)
Black pepper		
Black olives (optional)		

Scale and clean the fish and dust it with flour.

Heat a generous amount of olive oil in a pan with the garlic. Place the fish in the pan over high heat, and when the skin is sticky and lightly browned, turn the fish over carefully and brown the other side. Drain off the excess oil, remove the garlic, and add equal amounts of wine, broth, and tomatoes to the pan—just enough to come halfway up the sides of the fish. Season with salt and pepper. Sprinkle with parsley, add the olives if desired, cover the pan, and cook over very low heat until done. The fish is cooked if you are able to penetrate the meat with a fork all the way to the bone. If it is not fully cooked, it feels rubbery and stiff inside.

Once the fish is done, remove it from the pan and fillet it. Reduce the sauce over very high heat and serve it on top of the fish.

NOTE If you use canned tomatoes, add a pinch of sugar to reduce acidity.

TROTA SALMONATA ALL'ACETO BALSAMICO

COHO SALMON WITH BALSAMIC VINEGAR

*I*f Coho salmon is not available, you can use trout or baby salmon, common fish that you can find everywhere. Have the fish butterflied: this means the head stays on, the spine comes out, and the fish is cut through the stomach but not through the back. The marinade reaches the meat better this way. It is good baked, broiled, or grilled.

PANTRY	COLD STORAGE	MARKET
Balsamic vinegar		Coho salmon: 1 per person, butterflied
Olive oil		
Salt		
Crushed red pepper		

If you plan to bake the fish, preheat the oven to hot. Make a marinade of 1 part balsamic vinegar to 3 parts olive oil. Sprinkle the fish with salt and red pepper. Coat the fish flesh well with the marinade and let it rest in the mixture long enough to absorb the flavors—at least 30 minutes—turning occasionally.

Turn once again immediately before cooking and, with some of the marinade still clinging to the fish, broil, grill, or bake in a hot oven, skin side down, until a fork penetrates the meat easily.

TONNO ALLA LIVORNESE

TUNA STEAK, LIVORNESE STYLE

*T*una, or tonno *as we call it, is a big fish. I buy it for the restaurant in twenty-five-pound wheels, cut from the center, but even baby tuna is good. This recipe is also good for swordfish.*

PANTRY	COLD STORAGE	MARKET
Olive oil		Tuna: steaks cut 1 inch thick
White wine		
Canned tomatoes		
Capers		
Green olives		

Preheat the oven to medium. Cover the bottom of an ovenproof pan with a small amount of oil and sauté the tuna on both sides over high heat. When the tuna turns a light color, add wine halfway up the sides of the fish and continue to cook over high heat until the wine is reduced by half. Then add tomatoes, capers, and olives. Cover tightly, place in the oven, and cook slowly. Start to check with a fork after 10 minutes. The tuna is done when it flakes easily.

TONNACCIO AL PESTO E VINAGRETTE

GRILLED TUNA WITH A MARINADE OF PESTO AND VINAIGRETTE

PANTRY	COLD STORAGE	MARKET
Red wine vinegar	Lemons, cut in half	Fresh tomatoes, diced
Salt		Tuna: steaks cut at least 1 inch thick
Black pepper		
Olive oil		
Salsa al Pesto (recipe follows)		

To make the sauce, combine equal amounts of pesto and vinegar with 3 times the quantity of tomatoes. Add salt, pepper, and olive oil to taste. Mix well and set aside.

Wet the tuna with olive oil on both sides and broil it or grill it over hot coals until rare. Cut in thin slices and spread the sauce on top. Serve with lemon halves on the side.

SALSA AL PESTO
PESTO SAUCE

Make as much of this as you want—it keeps well in the refrigerator for several days, and it can be frozen for as long as you need. It can be served with many dishes—with pasta, cold or warm, with fish (preceding and following recipes), veal, shellfish, chicken, or salad. It should be served at room temperature or chilled, but never cooked.

PANTRY	COLD STORAGE	MARKET
Pignolis		Fresh basil leaves
Salt		
Black pepper		
Olive oil		

Separate the basil leaves from the stems, discard the stems, and wash the leaves. Grind the basil and pignoli nuts. Add salt and pepper to taste. Slowly pour in olive oil, mixing the sauce as you do so, until it reaches the consistency of green mud.

SOGLIOLA CON CAPPERI

SOLE WITH CAPERS

PANTRY	COLD STORAGE	MARKET
Salt	Butter	Sole: one 1-pound fish per person
Black pepper		Soybean oil
All-purpose flour		
Olive oil		
Capers		
White wine		
Salsa al Pesto (page 141)		

Preheat the oven to medium-hot. Clean the fish, or have it done at the fish market, but don't bone or fillet it. Dry fish well, season with salt and pepper, and dust both sides lightly with flour.

Pour enough olive oil in an ovenproof pan so that the fish won't stick, and when it is very hot add the sole. Braise on both sides until golden and pour out excess oil. Add a couple scoops of butter to the pan with the fish and, when the butter begins to melt, add about a teaspoon of pesto and a generous teaspoon of capers per fish. When the butter and pesto have melted together, add a splash of wine.

Cook fish just long enough for the wine to evaporate, then place the pan in the oven. Start to check after 5 minutes. Bake until you can pierce the fish to the bone with a fork and there is no resistance.

Remove sole to a warm platter and reduce the sauce over high heat. Bone the fish and serve with the warm sauce poured over it.

CEFALO ALLA DIAVOLA

DEVIL-STYLE MULLET

The last time I was in Italy I went to see my uncle and my aunt. She was preparing mullet, which wasn't in the refrigerator as it was supposed to be but was hanging, butterflied, in the window to dry—like underwear. She was preparing it the same way I had seen my grandmother do it for so many years. Time passes, but not so fast that these customs totally disappear.

Cefalo is a Mediterranean mullet. It makes up the largest population in the sea and it is to the legions of fish what the Chinese are to humanity. But even a common fish can have its own noble way of being cooked, its own way of tasting.

PANTRY	COLD STORAGE	MARKET
Olive oil		Small mullet: butterflied and dried or refrigerated
Salt		Italian fresh hot red pepper
		Fresh tomato, cut in half

Have mullet scaled, cleaned, and butterflied. Open it lengthwise but leave the skin intact. Then bone the fish and put it in the refrigerator for a few hours, uncovered, until the meat starts to get firm. Once this is done, the fun starts.

Break a red pepper in half and very gently brush the open side of the fish with the pepper, using the broken sides. As you brush, spread the seeds everywhere on the meat and squeeze the pepper so the juice comes out. Rub the cut side of each tomato half over the fish, squeezing out the juice, as you did with the pepper; then sprinkle with olive oil and salt.

Oil a broiling pan or grill and place the fish on it, skin side down. Cook until you can penetrate the fish with a fork to the spine and the fork comes out easily. Cook fish only on the skin side so the oil, tomato, salt, and pepper will be absorbed through the flesh. This dish has to be very spicy if it's to live up to its name—devil style.

VONGOLE ALLA MARINARA IN BIANCO

CLAMS STEAMED WITH GARLIC AND WHITE WINE

Here is a different way of cooking clams. For this recipe, use any type of clam you find at the market. From March all the way to September, a great variety is available—all types and all sizes. This is the kind of dish that, if you forget and leave it on the stove, nothing bad is going to happen. Use as many clams as you and your friends want to eat for lunch or a snack or dinner. I consider one pound of clams as two portions, no more.

PANTRY	COLD STORAGE	MARKET
Olive oil	Garlic, smashed	Cherrystone, Littleneck, or Manilla clams, soaked to remove sand
Crushed red pepper		
White wine		

In a deep pot, put a little bit of olive oil, garlic, and red pepper. When the oil is very, very hot and you can see the fumes coming out of the pot, that's the moment to add the clams. Be careful; stay back as you throw the clams in the pot and don't look inside because the oil will jump at your face. Add a glass of white wine, enough to wet the clams well. Cover, turn down the heat to medium, and let the clams steam until the shells have totally opened. Discard any that don't open. That's it. Serve them very hot and enjoy them.

VARIATION You can prepare mussels the same way. Sprinkle with some chopped fresh parsley before serving if you like.

MINESTRA DI GRANCHI

SOFT-SHELL CRAB SOUP

I have never forgotten the way my grandmother made this soup of crabs. It was pure heaven—thick and hearty. The soup can be made even heartier if you double the number of crabs and serve a whole crab floating in each person's bowl of soup. If you don't use whole crabs, add toasted garlic croutons on top. Better still, float a whole slice of Fettunta in each bowl. Then drizzle a little olive oil on top.

PANTRY	COLD STORAGE	MARKET
Olive oil	**Red onion, finely chopped**	**Soft-shell crabs: 1 or 2 per person**
Salt	**Garlic, smashed**	**Fresh thyme (see Note)**
Black pepper		
White wine (see Note)		
Canned tomatoes		

Fettunta (page 43)

Heat several tablespoons of olive oil in a large pot, add the onion and garlic, and sauté together over medium heat. When they have turned golden, add salt and pepper to taste. If you are using 2 crabs per person, cut half of them in quarters and add to the pot. Continue to cook over medium-high heat until they have absorbed the taste of the onion and garlic, then add the wine—as much as you need to completely cover the crabs, onion, and garlic. Turn the heat up very high and cook until some of the liquid evaporates. Add tomatoes and one of the most important ingredients, the fresh thyme, with the leaves stripped off the branches. Cover the ingredients in the pot with cold water and leave the heat high until the liquid begins to boil. Reduce the heat to medium-low, partially cover the pot, and let the soup cook for about 1 hour. A reddish foam will appear on top; this is the soft-shell crab releasing its liquid—and taste—to the sauce. It's fine.

Remove the chunks of soft-shell crab and puree them in a blender or food processor, then stir this mixture back into the soup. At this time, if you are using additional whole crabs, add them to the soup and allow them to cook through over low heat before serving. Serve over Fettunta.

NOTE Don't fool around with a cheap wine, or it will destroy the whole taste of the *minestra*. You need a very delicate white wine, a light Pitigliano Bianco or a very simple Trebbiano—very light, a little bit fruity, but dry, with no strong acidic component.

There are many varieties of thyme available. My favorite is lemon thyme, which has a yellow-pink flower, but the regular variety is fine. If necessary, use dried. The quantity is up to individual taste. I love the smell and taste of thyme, so I put a lot in.

A SMALL FISH STORY

My grandfather and uncles went fishing about five times a week, and when they came in they would take out the fish that were big enough to be sold and put them to one side. The small ones were their own provisions. They may have wanted to eat the big fish, but of course they were not going to touch anything they could sell, so my grandfather would take home many varieties of small fish—bavose, scorfani, paraghi, and all the others most nonfishermen would look at and say, "What the devil is this?"

My grandmother made a soup of them. She would take the heads off the fish and separate the bavose, the tastiest ones, from the others. She would sauté them with chopped garlic, onions, and parsley, then add a little water and almost forget about them. She didn't worry because she knew that the longer they cooked, the more juicy and flavorful they would be even if they fell apart.

Then she took the other small fish, cleaned them, took the heads off, removed the stomachs, rinsed them, and put them aside. At this point, she added tomato sauce and water to the bavose and continued to cook them. She never put the other small fish in until the soup was almost ready.

My grandfather used to call this dish the "Half-Carafe-of-Wine-in-Between" because, in between the time he brought the fish home and the soup was ready, he had enough time to go down to the vineria (a bar for drinking only wine), drink half a carafe, and get home again in time to eat.

When he came in the door, my grandmother would add the small fish to the bavose, which she had already ground up with the tomatoes, cook the mixture for just a few minutes longer, and serve the soup with a slice of garlic bread. The whole thing took less than an hour to make.

Fishermen know that small fish can be much more delicious than big ones. They managed to keep this a secret for a long time for two reasons: first, they needed those fish to feed their stomachs; and second, the rich thought the small fish looked ugly and didn't want to eat them because they had too many bones. Today in Tuscany, small fish are more popular than big ones. They can be made into a soup, and they can be fried quickly because the flesh is young and tender.

Small fish have always been popular with the lower and middle classes, but the rich are not stupid. They found out.

ALICI ALL'OLIO

ANCHOVIES IN OLIVE OIL

Especially in the summer, this dish is very refreshing, and it's excellent with a piece of Fettunta. It's the kind of dish that I could eat all day long.

PANTRY	COLD STORAGE	MARKET
Salt	Garlic, thinly sliced	Fresh anchovies, filleted and butterflied
Red wine vinegar or lemon juice	Fresh parsley, chopped	
Olive oil		
Crushed red pepper		
Fettunta (page 43)		

Put the anchovies in a shallow dish, sprinkle them with salt, and pour in enough vinegar or lemon juice to cover them. Marinate for at least 1 hour.

Pour off the vinegar or lemon juice and put the anchovies into another shallow dish. As you move them, let all the excess liquid drip off. Make a layer of anchovies, scatter garlic slices on top of them, and sprinkle with olive oil, red pepper, and parsley. Put another layer of anchovies on top and continue layering. Refrigerate until ready to serve with the Fettunta.

ALICI GRATINATE

GRATINÉED ANCHOVIES

PANTRY	COLD STORAGE	MARKET
Olive oil	Garlic, chopped	Anchovies, cleaned and butterflied
Bread crumbs	Fresh parsley, chopped	Rosemary (fresh, if possible)
White wine		

Preheat the oven to medium. Rub the inside of a baking dish with a generous amount of olive oil and put the anchovies into the dish. In another bowl, mix together the garlic, parsley, a little bit of rosemary, and the bread crumbs. We call this mixture *battutino*. Sprinkle it over the anchovies and add a little wine to the baking dish. Bake about 10 minutes and serve hot.

SARDE FRITTE

FRIED SARDINES

PANTRY	COLD STORAGE	MARKET
All-purpose flour	Eggs	Sardines, heads off, filleted and butterflied
Salt	Lemons, cut in half	
Black pepper		
Bread crumbs		
Olive oil		

Beat the eggs with a fork. Dry off the sardines. Dust the sardines with flour, salt, and pepper, then dip them in beaten eggs and then in bread crumbs. Fry in olive oil until firm and crunchy—as simple as that. Serve with lemons on the side.

SARDE AL VINO BIANCO

SARDINES IN WHITE WINE

*S*arde *are huge sardines; "sardines" are the small ones. I love them both. But in this recipe I suggest the big ones because they don't fall apart in cooking. This recipe is also good with fresh anchovies.*

PANTRY	COLD STORAGE	MARKET
Olive oil	Garlic, smashed	Large sardines, heads off, filleted and butterflied
White wine	Fresh parsley, chopped	
Salt		
Black pepper		

Cover the bottom of a pan with olive oil and sauté the garlic over medium heat until golden. Remove garlic and add the sardines in a single layer. Sauté them for a minute or two over medium heat; they cook very quickly so don't let the heat get too high. Drain off the excess oil and add enough wine to barely cover. Cook over medium heat for just a minute to reduce wine somewhat, not too long or sardines will break apart. Sprinkle sardines with parsley, salt, and pepper. Cover the pan tightly and let the sardines cook for about 2 minutes over very low heat. Don't turn them over while they are cooking or they may break. That's it.

VARIATION For SARDE AL POMODORO E BASILICO (Sardines with Tomatoes and Basil), prepare sardines the same as above, only add canned plum tomatoes and basil at the same time as the salt and pepper.

A MEAL BY THE SEA

The local people who live along the coast of Tuscany make a fish stew called Cacciucco. This dish is popular from Porto Santo Stefano in the south all the way to Livorno in the north. The beaches along this coastline are bordered by a dark and thick pine woods, unbroken except for a few open areas. The locals go to these areas to fish. At one time there was a wooden bungalow near Castiglion delle Pescaia—a one-room house with a big chimney. In it lived an old fisherman, a pescatore. This fisherman had his own small business making Cacciucco. At sunset he put down the nets and in the morning took them out and prepared the fish for the Cacciucco. In the winter he worked on a fishing boat for a big Italian company, but in the summer he cooked Cacciucco from his own bungalow. He had some tables beneath the overhang of his roof so diners could sit in the shade while they ate. He served it in pottery bowls, and I always wondered where he washed them—probably in sea water, which in that area is clean and pure.

If you got there and no Cacciucco was ready, you didn't mind waiting because the beach was right there and you could just lie down on the sand with a glass of the local wine. Between the sun and the wine you usually fell asleep, but you knew when your Cacciucco was ready because the smell woke you up.

He cooked the Cacciucco in a huge iron pot over a wood fire outside his bungalow. He poured some oil in this pot, then added garlic and onions, and let them cook until they were almost burnt. He started with crabs, mussels, and clams, then added big chunks of fish, eel, rockfish—whatever he had. Then the other fish were put in according to size, with the small fish and shrimp left for last. He added plum tomatoes—the kind that grow like wildfire all over Tuscany—and lots of parsley. When the tomatoes started to melt together with the fish and the seasonings, and the smell started to come on strong, he covered everything with cold water and let it cook. Twenty minutes later you were in heaven.

I was young and it was great to go there in summer and have my lunch for a couple thousand lire. Years later, I went back and looked for him, but nobody was there. You could still see traces of the fires he had built, but the poor guy had died. The sad thing is there was nobody to replace him, and his Cacciucco was so good.

IL CACCIUCCO

FISH AND BREAD STEW, TUSCAN STYLE

PANTRY	COLD STORAGE	MARKET
Olive oil	Garlic, chopped	Shellfish, including clams, mussels, and shrimp, cleaned and left in their shells
Salt	Red onions, coarsely chopped	
Black pepper		
Fettunta (page 43)	Fresh parsley, chopped	Fish, a large variety, including eel and small fish, boned and cut into chunks
		Tomatoes (fresh or canned)

Cover the bottom of a large pot with plenty of olive oil, add the onions and garlic, and sauté them over medium heat until golden. Add clams and mussels. (Everything that is strong tasting and juicy goes in the pot first.) Next add the chunks of eel and the rest of the fish according to size—the larger ones first, then the smaller ones. And then add the shrimp. Let everything cook briefly over high heat. Season with salt and pepper and add the tomatoes. (If you are using canned tomatoes, break them into chunks and add them with their juice. If you are using fresh tomatoes, quarter them.) Add parsley, putting a small amount aside for garnish. Let everything cook until hot, then cover the mixture with cold water to stop the cooking. Bring back to a simmer and cook over low heat, uncovered, until the fish is tender. Be careful not to overcook. Start to check the mixture after it has been simmering for 10 minutes to see if the fish is cooked. If you can penetrate it easily with a fork, it is done.

Once the Cacciucco is cooked (which doesn't take very long because you don't want the fish to get soft and break apart), put a piece of Fettunta in each bowl, spoon the stew over it shells and all, and sprinkle with parsley.

CALAMARI ALLA PESCATORA

SQUID, FISHERMAN'S STYLE

PANTRY	COLD STORAGE	MARKET
Olive oil	Garlic, smashed	Squid
Salt		Green peas, parboiled
Crushed red pepper		
White wine		
Canned tomatoes		

To prepare the squid, separate the tentacles from the sack, then remove the eyes and discard them. Rinse the tentacles well under running water. With your fingers, remove the inner membrane from the sack and any skin, cartilage, bones, or other material and discard. Rinse the sack under running water. Dry the sack and tentacles well; slice the sack into thin rings and cut the tentacles into small, 1- to 2-inch pieces.

Put a little bit of olive oil in a frying pan and add 1 or 2 cloves of garlic and the squid. Add the salt and red pepper and cook over high heat. Once the squid starts to cook, it will become very white and release its water. If there is excess liquid, pour it out. At this point, add a generous glass of wine and the tomatoes.

Continue to cook over very high heat for several minutes, then turn the heat down, cover the pan, and continue to cook until the squid is very tender. Start to check after about 15 or 20 minutes, and if the squid can be penetrated easily with a fork, it is done. At the end of the cooking, add the peas and simmer everything for a few more minutes. Adjust seasonings, and if you feel that there is not enough wine—that the taste isn't coming out strong enough or the dish isn't moist enough —add a little more. Turn up the heat and, with the pan uncovered, reduce the sauce a bit. Serve immediately with good crusty bread to soak up the sauce.

CALAMARI RIPIENI
ALLA FIORENTINA
STUFFED SQUID, FLORENTINE STYLE

PANTRY	COLD STORAGE	MARKET
Salt	Garlic, finely chopped	Squid
Black pepper	Lemons: juice, grated peel, and wedges	Spinach, boiled, squeezed dry, and chopped
Olive oil		

If you plan to bake the squid, preheat the oven to hot. Prepare the squid as described in the preceding recipe. Keep the body of the squid whole, and chop the tentacles into tiny pieces. Combine the tentacle pieces, garlic, spinach, salt and pepper, olive oil, lemon juice, and lemon peel. Mix well, taste, and if the flavor seems right, stuff this mixture into the body of the squid. Don't force it in—just fill it gently. You can leave the squid open, as it is, or use toothpicks to hold the mixture in.

Sprinkle with olive oil and a little salt, then put the squid in the oven, under the broiler, or on the grill. If you use the broiler, make sure the squid doesn't burn. Use medium heat and turn gently to brown all sides. The filling won't come out if you haven't packed the body too full. The squid is done when the body plumps up and you can penetrate it easily with a fork. Serve with lemon wedges on the side.

CALAMARI IN ZIMINO
SQUID AND SPINACH

PANTRY	COLD STORAGE	MARKET
Olive oil		Squid
Canned tomatoes		Spinach, washed, chopped, and parboiled
Salt		
Crushed red pepper		
Odori (page 30)		

Prepare the squid according to the directions on page 152. Sauté the odori in olive oil over medium heat until golden, then add an equal quantity of tomatoes, season with salt and red pepper, and cook for several minutes, still over medium heat. Add the squid, partially cover the pot, and let the mixture simmer. Check for doneness in about 20 minutes. If it gets too dry, add water.

In a separate bowl, mix a little olive oil and salt into the cooked, drained spinach. Ten minutes before serving the squid, mix in the spinach and let simmer together to flavor each other.

POLPO ALLA GRIGLIA
GRILLED OCTOPUS

PANTRY	COLD STORAGE	MARKET
Olive oil	Red onion, finely chopped	Octopus, not over ½ pound each
Salt	Fresh parsley, chopped	
Black pepper	Lemon juice and wedges	

Bring a large pot of water to a boil, add the octopus, and boil until tender. Start to check after about 15 or 20 minutes; if the octopus can be easily pierced with a fork, it is done.

Meanwhile, make the sauce by mixing equal amounts of onion and parsley. Add a bit of lemon juice to this mixture, but go easy on the lemon juice

—you don't want it to overpower the sauce. Add enough olive oil to cover the mixture.

Drain the octopus. While it is still hot, soak it in the sauce. Then put the octopus under the broiler or on the grill. Start to check the octopus after 2 to 3 minutes. When it begins to get brown and firm, it's ready. Serve with a little extra olive oil on top and lemon wedges on the side.

POLPETTI IN UMIDO

BABY OCTOPUS STEW

If you find small to medium octopus in the fish market, prepare them this way—in a stew. If only the large octopus are available, you can steam them first and then grill them (see Polpo alla Griglia, above). In either case, clean the octopus in the same way: first rinse them in fresh water and then remove the outer membrane.

PANTRY	COLD STORAGE	MARKET
Olive oil	Garlic, chopped	Octopus, cleaned
Salt	Red onion, chopped	
Black pepper		
Dry white wine (good-quality)		
Canned tomatoes		
Fettunta (page 43)		

Cover the bottom of a pan with olive oil and sauté garlic and onion over medium heat until golden. Add the octopus, salt, and pepper, mix well and let everything cook over high heat. Add white wine—enough to barely cover. Let the wine evaporate, then add enough tomatoes, mashed in their own juice, to cover the octopus mixture. Turn the heat down and let mixture cook, partially covered. Check for doneness in about 45 minutes.

At this point you have 2 choices: eat the stew directly from the pan with a slice of Fettunta to soak up the sauce, or put the octopus and sauce over Fettunta on a plate.

SEPPIE NERE IN UMIDO
BLACK CUTTLEFISH STEW

*C*uttlefish is very similar to squid. The only difference is that when you separate the two parts of the cuttlefish, you find on one side a small black sac which contains the ink. Be sure the cuttlefish you buy has not had the ink sacs removed.

PANTRY	COLD STORAGE	MARKET
Olive oil	Red onion, chopped	Cuttlefish
White wine	Garlic, chopped	
Polenta (page 87)	Fish or vegetable broth (optional)	

Separate the sacs with the ink and keep them on the side. Clean and prepare the cuttlefish as for Risotto Nero alle Seppie (page 127). Don't confuse the sacs with the eyes.

Rinse the cuttlefish very well and cut them in pieces if they are big. (If they are small you can leave them whole.) Sauté the onion and garlic in olive oil over medium heat until golden, then add the cuttlefish. Turn the heat up to high and mix well to coat the cuttlefish with olive oil. Then add broth or water and wine to cover. Continue cooking over high heat until the liquid starts to boil. Turn the heat down a bit, keeping the mixture at a simmer.

Meanwhile, combine the ink sacs with a bit of hot water and mash the sacs with a spoon so you obtain a very black liquid. When the cuttlefish has cooked for about 45 minutes and the liquid is reduced, add the ink and continue cooking for another 15 minutes.

My favorite way to serve this is with a firm Polenta that you've made in advance. Put the Polenta on the plate and the cuttlefish and black sauce on top. This is very good.

LUMACHE IN UMIDO
SNAIL STEW

During my many years of traveling up and down Italy as an actor, I found the cooking of Tuscany was always my favorite. This is not owing to any regional loyalty, but because of the simplicity of the food that was offered in any small village in the middle of nowhere, whether near Siena, Arezzo, and Florence or Lucca or Pisa. It was always different, and always distinctively Tuscan. For example, consider the way snails are prepared in Tuscany. They are buried deep in ashes for two or three days to clean them, then they are stewed in a fresh tomato sauce with garlic and onions, helped out of their shells with tiny toothpicks, and served with a glass of nice red wine. If the season is spring, they can be eaten with scallions. This dish is not rich or heavy, but offers a level of pleasure that you can't have with more complicated foods.

PANTRY	COLD STORAGE	MARKET
Nutmeg	Red onions, finely chopped	Fresh snails
Salt		Fresh thyme
Black pepper	Beef, chicken, or vegetable broth	
Olive oil		
Red wine		
Canned tomatoes		

If you're using fresh snails and you want to clean them as they do in Tuscany, let them sit in wood ashes or, if that's impossible, flour. Then soak them in several changes of salted water until all the slime and flour or wood ashes are removed.

Take a nice quantity of thyme, a little bit of nutmeg, the onions, salt, and pepper and put them in a pan with olive oil. Let this get very hot and then toss in the snails. Let snails absorb the taste of the herbs and the oil, so all the flavors go in the cavities.

At this point, add some broth and red wine in the same proportion. Continue to cook over high heat and let the wine and broth evaporate somewhat, then reduce the heat and add a very little bit of tomatoes mashed in their own juice—just enough to give the snail sauce a reddish color. Cover the pan and cook for at least 20 minutes.

The only things you need are a shallow bowl for the snails, some toothpicks, and a thick piece of bread to dip in the sauce.

GAMBERI ALLA GRIGLIA
GRILLED SHRIMP

Although every region of Italy has a different name for them, in Tuscany, shrimp are called gamberi *or* cicale. *And in Tuscany we are primitive, so we don't like shrimp out of the shell. We keep them with their cover, the way they come from the sea.*

When shrimp are fresh, particularly the big ones, place them belly up and slice down the middle, just enough to cut through the shell, which is strong and hard. Hold the skin open a little bit, season the flesh with salt and pepper, drizzle some olive oil on top, and put them on the grill or under the broiler for a minute or two to cook.

Cooking shrimp in the shell has a purpose. It keeps the taste of seawater and salt between the shell and the meat. This seawater taste comes out very sweet from the meat and very salty from the sea.

If you want to enjoy shrimp, eat them hot, as soon as they come from the broiler, full of fragrance. When you can stand the heat of the shell, break it with your hand, take off the head, and suck out the juice, which is very, very good. You'll get a little messy when you eat shrimp this way, but if you use baby forks to eat them, they will get cold. Just pull the meat out with your fingers and squeeze the shell. The juice is there.

With gamberi, *you don't have to eat a lot to have great taste and flavor. Have them with a nice salad and a glass of wine. When shrimp are in season for reproduction, there are eggs inside and I'm telling you, caviar can't compare with the taste of this roe! I buy Monterey prawns with the roe from California. I could eat three pounds right now.*

PANTRY	COLD STORAGE	MARKET
Salt		Extra-large shrimp, preferably with heads on
Black pepper		
Olive oil		

Belly up, slice the shrimp down the middle, cutting through the shell and into the flesh no more than ¼ inch deep. Rub inside and out with salt, pepper, and olive oil. Place on grill or under broiler. Turn once and continue cooking until flesh is white. *Caution:* Watch carefully, since these take only a minute or so to cook.

GAMBERI ALLA PESCATORA

SHRIMP, FISHERMAN'S STYLE

PANTRY	COLD STORAGE	MARKET
Olive oil	Garlic, smashed	Shrimp, in or out of the shell
Salt	Fresh parsley, chopped	
White wine		
Canned tomatoes		
Black pepper		

Cover the bottom of a pan with olive oil and sauté garlic over medium heat until golden. Remove garlic, add shrimp, and continue to sauté until they turn white. Pour off extra olive oil, then add a pinch of salt and enough wine to just cover. Continue to cook over medium heat and, when the wine is reduced somewhat, add tomatoes, parsley, and pepper. Partially cover and cook 5 minutes or so over medium-low heat.

SCAMPI IMPANATI ALLA GRIGLIA

BREADED AND BROILED SHRIMP

PANTRY	COLD STORAGE	MARKET
Bread crumbs	Lemon juice and wedges	Large shrimp, out of their shells
Olive oil	Fresh parsley, minced	
Salt		
Black pepper		

Preheat the oven to medium. Place bread crumbs in a bowl and mix with enough olive oil to moisten well. Add lemon juice and salt and pepper to taste. Stir in parsley. Roll shrimp in mixture until well coated. Layer shrimp in an oiled casserole and spread a little of the leftover bread crumbs on the top. Sprinkle with olive oil and bake for about five minutes or until the crumbs form a golden crust. Place under the broiler briefly to brown. Serve with lemon wedges.

LA CACCIAGIONE

HUNTING FOR GAME

Tuscans are called "bean-eaters," but they probably eat as much game as they do beans. In fact, Tuscans are the greatest eaters of game in Italy.

I've always been attracted to game because it reminds me of the Middle Ages. Although it was one of the darkest periods in human history, the stories and paintings that have come to us from that time make it seem romantic and voluptuous. The villages, the castles, and the dining halls are so vivid to me that I can see them filled with soldiers, barons, and dukes eating huge quantities of game at long wooden tables, with quail, pheasant, rabbit, venison, and wild boar roasting on spits over a strong, raw fire.

It wasn't until the Renaissance that more elaborate dishes were developed. In Montalcino, Emma Primo still makes the Renaissance dishes that have been in her family for three or four hundred years. This cooking is called the Cucina delle Ville, which means "Cuisine for the Villas"—the traditional dishes that have been served for years to the aristocrats who live in the big villas of Tuscany.

The last time I saw Emma, she was preparing a dinner for thirty people. She had to start in August for a dinner in September. The meal begins with piatti di credenza, which means "dishes coming from the credenza": salami, prosciutti, formàggi—everything stored in the hutch comes out first. Next, she brings out the antipasti di cucina, which is any kind of vegetable marinated in oil or preserved in vinegar. Then comes the real beginning of the meal—a selection of soups and broth. She makes the broth from game—wild boar, hare, and pigeon —and she saves the meat from the broth to make pâté and cold appetizers for future meals. Next comes the pasta course, then the main course, which always includes animals that are stuffed. If you look at certain Renaissance paintings, you'll see how this was done. There are pigs stuffed with apples, wild boars stuffed with vegetables, and pheasants stuffed with birds that have been stuffed with oysters. All these stuffed animals resulted in an extremely elaborate but redundant presentation.

In the Renaissance, combining game and seafood was done only by the rich. The aristocrats knew that peasants ate game and fishermen ate fish, but the combination of these tastes was the invention of the aristocrat, and access to products from both the earth and the sea was a luxury available only to them.

Page 160: **La selvaggina (game market)**

ANATRA AL VERMOUTH SECCO

DUCK WITH DRY VERMOUTH

One of my favorite dishes is duck. The only trouble is that duck is a very fatty bird. To defat it, I use a cone-shaped vertical roaster made of wire, with a pan underneath to catch the fat. (These roasters can be found in specialty shops and some department stores.)

This is a very simple recipe, and believe me, it's delicious. Whenever I make it at the restaurant, it doesn't last long. I have to put a duck aside for myself or I won't get any. I love it.

PANTRY	COLD STORAGE	MARKET
Salt		Duck (mallard, Muscovy, or Pekin), cleaned and interior removed
Black pepper		
Olive oil		
Dry vermouth		

Preheat the oven to medium. Season duck with salt and pepper, place in a vertical roasting pan or roaster, and place in the oven. (If you are not using the vertical roaster, prick the duck skin in several places to release the fat as it cooks.)

When the skin starts to get crisp, put a bit of olive oil on it to keep it from getting too dry. Check for doneness in about an hour. When the duck feels tender when pierced with a fork and the juices run clear, remove it, leaving the oven on.

Let the duck cool somewhat and cut it into quarters. Return it to the oven just until the duck is very hot again. Remove it from the oven and immediately pour over the duck as much vermouth as it can absorb. Whatever sauce is left on the bottom of the pan, pour over the duck again before serving.

ANATRA ALL'ARANCIA
DUCK WITH ORANGE SAUCE

This dish originated in Italy rather than France, as many people think. It was brought from Florence to France by Catherine de Medici when she married Henry II in 1533.

PANTRY	COLD STORAGE	MARKET
Olive oil	Red onions, finely chopped	Duck (mallard, Muscovy, or Pekin), cut into chunks with interior removed
White wine	Chicken or vegetable broth	
Salt		Oranges: peel of 1 orange, finely chopped; juice of 2 or 3 oranges; 1 orange, sliced
Black pepper		
Sugar		

Preheat the oven to medium. Cover the bottom of a pan with olive oil and place over high heat. Add the duck and brown it, turning it as it browns. Lower the heat to medium, prick the skin with a fork in several places, and cook slowly for about 5 minutes to allow the duck to lose its fat.

Dampen the bottom of an ovenproof pan with olive oil and place over medium heat. Add the onions and the duck and cook uncovered until all the flavors combine and the onions become soft. Add just enough broth and wine, in equal amounts, to cover the duck, along with the chopped orange peel, juice, salt, and pepper.

Place the pan in the oven, cover, and roast, starting to test for doneness after about 1 hour. When the duck feels tender and the juices run clear when pierced with a fork, stir a spoonful of sugar and the sliced orange into the pan juices. Serve the sauce with the duck.

FAGIANO ALLA CACCIATORA

PHEASANT, HUNTER'S STYLE

Among the many kinds of game you can eat, pheasant is one of the most delicious. It is also one of the easiest to hunt because the poor fellow can't fly as well as he can run.

PANTRY	COLD STORAGE	MARKET
Salt	Chicken or vegetable broth	Pheasant, about 2 to 3 pounds
Black pepper		
Olive oil		
Red wine		
Canned tomatoes		
Odori (page 30)		

Preheat the oven to medium. Cut pheasant in pieces and season with salt and pepper. Sauté odori in olive oil over medium heat in an ovenproof pan until full of color. Add pheasant and brown on all sides. Turn up the heat, add 2 or 3 glasses of wine, and cook until the wine evaporates. Add enough tomatoes to cover the pheasant comfortably but not drown it.

Lower the heat, cover the pan, and roast in the oven. If the pheasant becomes too dry, add broth, wine, or tomatoes—whichever you prefer. Start to check for doneness after about 20 minutes by piercing the bird with a fork. When the juices run clear, the pheasant is done.

QUAGLIE ARROSTO
AL TARRAGONE
ROASTED QUAIL WITH TARRAGON

Besides rosemary, we have lots of tarragon in Tuscany. People who live along the Tuscan coast use it in everything. It's such a common herb that I doubt if most of the people in Tuscany even know its name; I didn't when I lived there.

Quail dishes are appropriate for any occasion—if you are having a business dinner, dinner with your boyfriend or girlfriend, or, if you are a pope, with your clerico. Whatever. From October to March, it is always possible to find fresh quail, especially Canadian quail. Stay with very small quail and don't eat the bay leaf.

PANTRY	COLD STORAGE	MARKET
Salt	Chicken or vegetable broth, if needed	Quail (Canadian or European), 2 per person, interiors removed
Black pepper		
Olive oil		
1 bay leaf per bird		Fresh tarragon
		Pancetta (Italian thick-sliced bacon), 2 slices per bird

Preheat the oven to medium-hot. Season quail inside and out with salt and pepper; rub them with olive oil. Stuff the inside of each bird with tarragon, place a bay leaf on the breast, and wrap each quail with 2 or 3 slices of pancetta to hold the herbs in place. Put the birds in a pan large enough to hold all of them and pour enough oil in to cover them. Marinate for several hours, turning them several times in the oil.

Drain excess oil from the birds and place them in the oven. Keep an eye on the quail as they bake, and if they get too dry, baste them with broth—this will help them make their own gravy. Start to test them for doneness after about 10 minutes by piercing the quail with a fork. When the juices run clear, the skins are golden, and the chests are proud, the quail are done. Run under the broiler to crisp the bacon before serving.

QUAGLIE E SALSICCIA CON POLENTA

QUAIL AND SAUSAGE WITH POLENTA

PANTRY	COLD STORAGE	MARKET
Olive oil	Red onions, thinly sliced	Fresh sweet and hot Italian sausages, peeled and cut in half lengthwise, ½ sausage each per person
Salt		
Black pepper	Chicken or vegetable broth, if needed	
Red wine		
Canned tomatoes		Quail (Canadian or European), 2 per person
Polenta (page 87)		

Preheat the oven to medium. Heat a small amount of olive oil in an ovenproof pan; add onions and cook until soft over low heat. Drain off any excess oil, add the sausages, and cook over low heat until they lose their fat and break apart. Pour off all but a slight film of fat on the bottom of the pan and add the quail. Let them cook with the sausage and onions over high heat until the quail take on color. Taste for salt and pepper. Add a glass of wine, lower the heat, and let the sausage and birds cook until the wine is absorbed. Add the tomatoes and place the pan, covered, in the oven. In about 30 minutes, pierce the birds with a fork to test for tenderness; when the quail are done, the juices will run clear.

Prepare the Polenta while the quail are roasting (it should have a firm consistency). Put the quail and sausages on the Polenta and cover with the sauce. If the Polenta gets cold while the quail are cooking, add a little broth and stir briefly over low heat. It should remain moist—not too liquid, but not too dry. Serve the quail with the pan juices.

PICCIONE IN UMIDO CON FUNGHI

SQUAB STEW WITH MUSHROOMS

*P*iccione *is wild pigeon, or squab. The medium size is the best—not too big, not too small—and definitely not the one that comes from Central Park (or salmonella is the first thing that's going to happen to you).*

A squab is a very particular kind of bird, with very gamy meat. It's not the kind of food I suggest to people who are touchy about game, because the taste of squab is really one of the roughest. Marination is necessary to make the squab meat more tender.

I serve one squab per person. Remember also that recipes for squab are also good for partridge.

PANTRY	COLD STORAGE	MARKET
Olive oil	Butter	Squab, with interiors if available, otherwise chicken livers
Salt	Red onions, thinly sliced	
Black pepper		Fresh sage
Red wine	Chicken or vegetable broth	
Canned tomatoes		Cultivated mushrooms, cremini, or any mild mushroom, thinly sliced
Marinata per Selvaggina (page 170)		

Marinate the squab overnight but not longer than 24 hours. The next day, cut birds in half down the middle. Remove the interiors and cut the squab into quarters. Sauté the interiors over high heat in butter and sage, chop them, and set aside.

In another pan, heat the olive oil and add the mushrooms, onions, salt and pepper to taste, the chopped interiors, squab, and enough wine and broth to come halfway up the sides of the squab. Cook over very high heat until some of the liquid has evaporated.

Add the tomatoes, partially cover, turn the heat to very low, and let simmer until the squab are tender when pierced with a fork. Start to check after 15 minutes. Do not overcook because when game cooks too long it becomes tough.

If there is too much liquid in the pan when the squab are done, remove the squab and reduce the liquid over very high heat. Put the squab back in the reduced sauce, reheat, and serve.

PICCIONE IN SALMI

SQUAB, SALMI STYLE

PANTRY	COLD STORAGE	MARKET
Black olives (Gaeta or Niçoise), some pitted and chopped, some left whole	Butter	Squab, with interiors if available, otherwise, use chicken livers
Olive oil	Red onion, thinly sliced	Fresh sage
Red wine	Chicken or vegetable broth	
Marinata per Selvaggina (page 170)		

Marinate squab overnight but not longer than 24 hours. The next day, remove interiors, chop them, and sauté in butter and sage over high heat until brown. (Don't worry if the butter turns brown or even black —it should). Mix in the chopped olives and stuff this mixture into the cavities of the squab. Sew the birds closed and set aside.

Preheat the oven to hot. In a large ovenproof pan, sauté the onion in olive oil over medium heat until soft. Add the stuffed squab to the pan and cook slowly until they absorb the taste of the olive oil and onion, about 3 or 4 minutes. Cover the birds with roughly equal amounts of wine and broth and add some whole olives. Cover and roast in the oven. Start to check for doneness after about 10 minutes by piercing the birds with a fork. When the juices run clear, they are done.

MARINATA PER SELVAGGINA

MARINADE FOR SQUAB AND RABBIT

*S*ome of the game I serve in the restaurant could be too strong for American taste, and that's why I marinate it—to refine the flavor. Sometimes I do so much marinating that I begin to wonder what I started with. I adjust recipes to make the meats less raw, less rough, and then I feel I'm betraying my roots because I'm calling these dishes by their Tuscan names, but I haven't made them in the way they are really eaten in Tuscany. Of course, I always adjust recipes when my instincts tell me that changing something will make it better. That's in the creative spirit of cooking. Sometimes when people taste strong flavors they think there's a problem with it, but it could be the other way around. It's not because the food isn't "sophisticated"; it's that we, perhaps, are not civilized enough to appreciate it.

PANTRY	COLD STORAGE	MARKET
Red wine	Red onion, finely chopped	Squab or rabbit
Juniper berries	Carrot, finely choped	
	Celery , finely chopped	

Put the squab or rabbit in a large bowl and cover with wine. Add the onion, carrot, celery, and juniper berries. Marinate in the refrigerator for not more than a day, turning it several times in the marinade.

CONIGLIO IN FRICASSEA

RABBIT FRICASSÉE

Rabbit is not exclusively fall game; you can have it all year round. You know rabbits. Every week you get a new rabbit. The important thing is size. A three-and-a-half- or four-pound rabbit is very good, but a three-pound rabbit is the best—the small to medium size.

With a fricassée I use sage because I like the combinations of sage and lemon and sage and cheese. My mother uses a lot of tarragon and she leaves out the cheese. Instead, she adds milk or cream and ties it all together with some butter. It depends on personal taste and which herbs you like. I like tarragon, but sage for rabbit is very, very good.

PANTRY	COLD STORAGE	MARKET
Olive oil	Red onions, finely chopped	Rabbit, cleaned and cut into pieces
Salt	Beef broth	Branches of fresh thyme and fresh sage, tied together
Black pepper	2 egg yolks, with a splash of milk added	
White wine		
Marinata per Selvaggina (preceding page)	Parmesan cheese, grated	
	Lemon juice	

Marinate the rabbit overnight but not longer than 24 hours. The next day, sauté the onions in olive oil over low heat until soft. Remove the rabbit from the marinade and dry thoroughly; add it to the pan, turn up the heat, and sauté until golden. Add salt and pepper, a glass of wine, and thyme and sage branches. Cover with broth and bring to a boil. Reduce the heat and cook very slowly, uncovered, until the rabbit is tender. Start to check for doneness in about 30 minutes. The rabbit is done when the meat is extremely tender and white.

Meanwhile, whip the egg yolks with a drop of milk and a touch of Parmesan cheese. Add a splash of lemon juice and more salt and pepper, if needed. When the stew is almost ready, remove the bundle of herbs, add the egg mixture, and cook for just a little while longer, until the heat of the rabbit has cooked the egg mixture and the stew has thickened slightly.

CONIGLIO ALLA CACCIATORA

RABBIT, HUNTER'S STYLE

In Tuscany, in the fall, I always think of rosemary. By the sea at this time of year, the water is very quiet; the light changes and the sea is smoother, less lively than in the summer. Nothing moves. The water looks like a blue tablecloth. And the smells change—that's the best part. Rosemary has a strong aroma in the fall. You can smell it everywhere you go on the coast.

PANTRY	COLD STORAGE	MARKET
Olive oil	Garlic, smashed	Rabbit, with interiors, cleaned and cut in pieces
White wine		
Salt		Fresh rosemary
Black pepper		
Marinata per Selvaggina (page 170)		

If you plan to roast the rabbit, preheat the oven to medium. Marinate the rabbit and interiors overnight but not longer than 24 hours. Slowly heat olive oil in a pan, add garlic, and sauté over medium heat until golden. Remove the garlic, and put the rabbit into the pan with the oil. Continue to cook over medium heat until the skin turns brown, but watch that it doesn't turn too brown; rabbit burns easily. Pour off the olive oil and add wine to cover. Turn up the heat to high and, when it is very hot, add rosemary, salt, pepper, and the interiors.

Partially cover the pan and turn down the heat. Cook very slowly until tender. Or, even better, put the pan in the oven. Either way, start to check the rabbit for doneness in about 30 minutes. The rabbit is ready when the meat is extremely tender and white. Slowly the rabbit will absorb the liquid and become tender, juicy, and flavorful. If you have too much liquid, remove the rabbit and reduce the liquid over high heat.

CONIGLIO IN UMIDO CON OLIVE NERE

RABBIT STEW WITH BLACK OLIVES

T*his recipe has so many variations, but here's one I particularly like. It's a very popular dish in the area between Siena and Grosseto, and my friend Giancarlo in Grosseto is known for making one of the best.*

PANTRY	COLD STORAGE	MARKET
Olive oil	Chicken or vegetable broth	Rabbit, cleaned and cut into pieces, with interiors
Salt		
Black pepper		Fresh tarragon
Red wine vinegar		Fresh thyme
Red wine (good-quality)		
Canned tomatoes		
Black olives, Gaeta or Niçoise		
Marinata per Selvaggina (page 170)		
Odori (page 30)		

Preheat the oven to medium. Marinate the rabbit and the interiors overnight but not longer than 24 hours. Mince the interiors. Cover the bottom of an ovenproof pan with olive oil. Turn the heat to medium and add the odori. Once it starts to color, add the interiors, a touch of salt and pepper, tarragon, and thyme. Turn the heat to high, add half a glass of vinegar and, when it evaporates, add the chunks of rabbit. When the rabbit has absorbed the flavor of the odori, vinegar, and herbs, cover it just barely with broth. Add a couple glasses of wine, a small amount of tomatoes smashed in their own juice, and the olives.

Continue to cook over high heat until the liquid is reduced, then cover and place in the oven. Start to check the rabbit for doneness in about 45 minutes. The rabbit is done when the meat is extremely tender and white.

CONIGLIO AL FORNO CON PATATE

ROAST RABBIT WITH POTATOES

*S*ome people may think a skinned rabbit is not nice to look at, but in some ways I find it rather funny. It is so naked looking, just flesh and bones. This simple recipe for roasted rabbit is juicy and pure heaven.

PANTRY	COLD STORAGE	MARKET
Olive oil	Garlic, cut into slivers	Rabbit, cleaned and left whole
Salt and black pepper	Lemon juice	Fresh rosemary
Marinata per Selvaggina (page 170)		New potatoes, in their skins

Marinate the rabbit and interiors overnight but not longer than 24 hours. Make gashes in the rabbit and force in slivers of garlic and sprigs of rosemary. Rub the rabbit with olive oil, sprinkle with lemon juice, and, if you have time, allow it to sit for at least 1 hour.

Place the rabbit in a roasting pan with the potatoes around it. Pour a generous amount of olive oil over all and season with salt, pepper, and more rosemary. Place in a moderate oven. If the rabbit is getting dry, add just enough cold water to help it retain its moisture. In about 30 to 45 minutes, start to check for doneness—the meat will be extremely tender and white.

CERVO AL MARSALA

VENISON WITH MARSALA WINE

PANTRY	COLD STORAGE	MARKET
All-purpose flour	Marinata per Cervo (recipe follows)	Medallions of venison, butterflied
Olive oil	Butter	Pearl onions, peeled and boiled until tender
Raisins		Dry Marsala wine
Pignolis		
Dried porcini, soaked in warm water and drained		
Salt and black pepper		

Marinate the venison overnight. Remove from the marinade, dry with paper towels, and pound flat. Dust venison with flour and shake off excess. Cover the bottom of a pan with olive oil and, when very hot, add venison. Brown quickly on both sides, then drain off oil completely. Add enough butter to moisten the bottom of the pan and put in the pearl onions, raisins, pignolis, and porcini. Season with salt and pepper. Add a generous splash of Marsala and turn heat up very high. Cook for about 30 seconds on each side. If sauce is too liquid, thicken it by adding a little butter. Remove medallions to plates and spoon sauce over them. Serve venison rare.

MARINATA PER CERVO

VENISON MARINADE

*V*enison is marinated not just to tenderize the meat but to take away the gamy taste. The longer you leave it in the marinade, the milder it will be. But don't marinate it longer than two days, or too much of the original taste will be lost. Refrigerate the meat while it marinates.

PANTRY	COLD STORAGE	MARKET
Red wine	Carrots, chopped	Venison, cut into chunks
Coriander seeds	Celery, chopped	
Red wine vinegar	Red onions, chopped	

Place the venison in a bowl just large enough to hold it comfortably. Add the chopped vegetables in equal proportion to the amount of venison and cover with red wine. Sprinkle with coriander seeds and add a generous splash of vinegar. Marinate the venison in the refrigerator, turning it occasionally in the marinade.

LE CARNI

STEWED,

ROASTED,

AND

GRILLED

MEAT

My friend Chicchero is a playwright and a screenwriter. He loves reading poetry and carries his favorite books with him all the time, much the way Linus carries his security blanket. James Joyce is always in his pocket; he has only to reach in once in awhile and read a paragraph aloud to make you think about a different way of life.

Several years ago, Chicchero and I and others were together on tour for six or seven months. We went to every part of Italy—north, west, east, south, up in the mountains, near the water, to small villages and big towns. After awhile, the focal point of the day was where we were going for dinner after the play. The play itself didn't count as much as the variety of food we found in different cities.

In a strange combination of fate and causality, we ended up working together in the same theater in Trieste. In Trieste there is a well-known wind called the Bora, which blows up to seventy or eighty miles an hour, but Trieste is a gorgeous city anyway. So one night when it was freezing and the Bora was blowing, four or five of us went out after the play to the only restaurant in Trieste that stayed open late. We ordered sweetbreads, oxtail stew, and veal shanks, turnips sautéed with onions, huge dumplings made with broth, and four or five bottles of red wine. The bottom line was that we were full of food and drink, and we left

Preceding pages and above: **Open-air meat market**

the restaurant knowing that we had to somehow walk back to the hotel. This was a big problem because Chicchero, when he was drunk, would go three steps forward and five steps back, all the time coming out with outrageous comments that would make you bend over your belly laughing just to look at him.

Because we were laughing, and he was happy that we were laughing, Chicchero was jumping all over us and kissing us everywhere he could reach us—on the neck, the ears, the eyes. It seems that we were making so much noise that someone called the police. My friend Marco and I tried to act sober and talk decently to the policeman when he arrived. We tried to tell him that we didn't mean to disturb anyone; we were just having a little fun. But because he was an Italian with a German officer's mentality, he decided to come to the hotel with us to get our papers. We only had to walk a hundred feet to the hotel, but we couldn't make it without laughing.

When we finally reached the door, with this officer following us, Chicchero turned around and said, "Thank you, officer, for escorting us." And gave him a big kiss on the eye. We finished the night in jail.

The day after, they let us out and we had to sign a paper saying we would appear in court. We never showed up. Maybe they're still looking for us, but more likely we got lost in the bureaucracy. That's Italy.

CODA ALLA VACCINARA

OXTAIL STEW

*I*t's nice to have a great oxtail stew waiting for you when it's cold and rainy outside. If you're having friends for dinner, start cooking the stew at least three hours before you're going to eat it. Just go out, see a movie, and forget about it. When you come home, sit down with a good bottle of wine—a Barolo, Barbaresco, Brunello—and the stew is ready. Serve it with a good bread to soak up the sauce and eat all the meat off the bone.

PANTRY	COLD STORAGE	MARKET
Corn oil	Red onions, chopped	Oxtails, in 1-inch pieces
All-purpose flour	Celery, chopped	
Olive oil	Garlic, chopped	
Red wine	Carrots, julienned	
Salt		
Black pepper		
Canned tomatoes		

Preheat the oven to hot. When you buy oxtail from a butcher, sometimes it's frozen, but that's okay; it doesn't change the dish that much. Remove the excess fat from the oxtail. Dust with flour. Heat corn oil in a large pan and brown the oxtail in the oil. When it is well browned and defatted, take it out, pour off the oil and fat, and let the oxtail drain in a colander.

Meanwhile, dampen the bottom of an ovenproof pan with olive oil and add onions, celery, and garlic. Sauté them over high heat until they have the characteristic, appetizing smell and their color is golden. Add the oxtail and keep mixing everything over very high heat to let the oxtail absorb the taste of the chopped vegetables. Now add the carrots and cook for 3 or 4 minutes over high heat.

Pour enough wine in the pot to cover the oxtail and bring it to the boiling point. (If you really want to make a successful dish, choose a good-quality red wine. In my restaurant, I use a young Chianti.) Then add salt and pepper—just a small quantity, because it's better to taste and add them at the end when the dish is almost ready. As soon as the dish reaches the boiling point, add a couple scoops of tomatoes.

Cover the pan and put it in the oven and immediately turn oven to moderate. The oxtail is ready when it is totally tender and falling off the bones, about 1½ to 2 hours. Separate the meat from the sauce and reduce the sauce a bit. Pour it over the meat and serve right away.

VARIATION Dried porcini, soaked in some of the red wine for the stew, can be added to the pan when you remove the oxtail and reduce the sauce. Strain and add the soaking liquid, too. Continue cooking 4 or 5 minutes over medium heat. This is a small but excellent variation on the recipe.

FEGATO ALLA SALVIA

CALF'S LIVER WITH SAGE

In order to make this dish very light, the liver must be sliced very thin. Make sure the liver you buy comes from a piece no bigger than six to eight pounds. That means it came from young cattle. If the liver is larger, the cattle are older and it may have a very sour taste. This recipe is one of those exceptions in Tuscan cooking, in which the butter is welcome.

PANTRY	COLD STORAGE	MARKET
All-purpose flour	Butter	Calf's liver, sliced very thin
		Fresh sage

Sprinkle some flour on a plate and dust the liver on both sides. Melt a generous scoop of butter in a frying pan and brown 4 or 5 sage leaves. Let the sage cook until it starts to burn. Add the calf's liver and sauté for 1 minute on one side, then 30 seconds on the other. I suggest that you cook each slice of liver separately. (Don't worry if the butter turns black. That's the natural reaction of the flour with the butter; it puts taste into the liver.)

ANIMELLE AL BURRO NERO E SALVIA

SWEETBREADS SAUTÉED IN BLACK BUTTER AND SAGE

Sweetbreads are an excellent dish—very rich, but very delicious. Fresh chicken livers or any interiors sautéed with browned butter and sage are also excellent.

PANTRY	COLD STORAGE	MARKET
Salt	Butter	Sweetbreads, peeled and presoaked
Black pepper		Fresh sage

Steam the sweetbreads in a steamer until they become white and opaque. Melt a generous scoop of butter in a frying pan and add the sweetbreads. Cook them slowly over low to medium heat so that the butter doesn't burn. When the sweetbreads are half done, add the sage and sprinkle the sweetbreads with salt and pepper. Cook for 2 or 3 minutes, until they are tender —pink in the center.

At the end of the cooking process, turn the heat up high for a few seconds. The butter will turn brown and react with the sweetbreads. You want to taste everything—the sweetbreads and the butter and the sage—as they all brown together.

BOLLITO MISTO

MIXED BOILED MEATS

PANTRY	COLD STORAGE	MARKET
Olive oil	Red onions, cut in half	Tongue, 2½ to 3 pounds
	Carrots	Chicken
	Celery	Eye round of beef
	Potatoes	

Put the tongue, chicken, and beef roast in 3 separate pots and cover each with water. Add the onions, a couple of carrots, and a couple stalks of celery to each pot. Bring each to a boil, then partly cover and turn the heat down to a simmer. Check the chicken for tenderness after about 30 minutes. The beef will take at least an hour, and the tongue at least 1½ hours. When the meats are tender, let the tongue cool, peel off the skin, slice it thinly, and set it aside. Slice the beef and set it aside. Save some of the water you've boiled the meats in and ladle a bit over the meats to keep them moist.

If desired, serve meats immediately, with the sauce spread on top. If serving later, cover each and keep cold. To reheat, put the meats back on the stove over low heat and let them warm up in the same water they cooked in. Put some tongue, beef, and chicken on each plate and spread Salsa Verde Piccante (recipe below) generously on top. Sprinkle on a little extra olive oil. Serve with boiled potatoes.

SALSA VERDE PICCANTE

PIQUANT GREEN SAUCE

This sauce can be made with many different ingredients, but this version is my favorite. It has to be very thick and very green, which means you must use plenty of parsley. The sauce keeps a long time, so don't worry about making too much. I like the strong taste of capers and boiled eggs, so I increase these amounts. Whatever you think will be good, you can add.

PANTRY	COLD STORAGE	MARKET
Anchovies, finely chopped	Hard-cooked eggs, chopped	Cornichons, finely chopped
Capers	Fresh parsley, chopped	
Salt	Garlic, finely chopped	
Black pepper	Lemon juice	
Olive oil		

Combine all ingredients except the olive oil and lemon juice. Add the lemon juice to taste and mix well. Then slowly add the olive oil—enough to smooth out the pungent taste. Add more salt and pepper, if needed.

STRACOTTO ALLA FIORENTINA

POT ROAST, FLORENTINE STYLE

*S*tracotto *means "overstewed." When you see the prefix* stra *in Italian, it means "too much," but here it doesn't have a negative meaning. This recipe, which originated in Florence, is very, very good.*

PANTRY	COLD STORAGE	MARKET
Salt	Garlic, smashed	Eye round of beef
Black pepper	Beef broth	
Olive oil		
Red wine		
Dried porcini, soaked in red wine		
Canned tomatoes		
Odori (page 30)		

Ask the butcher to trim all the extra fat from the meat, leaving just enough for braising. Preheat the oven to medium. Season the beef with salt and pepper. Use a snug oval pan if you can; otherwise, you'll have to use a lot of liquid. Dampen the bottom of the pan with a little olive oil. (The olive oil is not for cooking in this case; it's just to keep the meat from sticking.) Turn the heat up very high and brown the meat on all sides. There will be some smoke, but don't worry about it. The meat should be browned until it's practically burnt. The bottom of the pan will start to turn a dark color because the essence of the Stracotto, the fat and extra liquid, is collecting there. Don't get scared; that's the honey of the dish. It's important in creating the right taste.

Once the meat is brown, take it out of the pan and set it aside. In the same pan, place a thin layer of odori and the garlic. Brown them over high heat and add just enough wine to lift all the good stuff off the bottom of the pan. Put the meat back in the pan, set it over high heat, and let it absorb the scent and taste of the vegetables. After a minute, when you see the vegetables sticking to the meat, add wine or broth—or both—to cover the meat. (Use about 1 bottle of wine for 4 people because a lot of wine evaporates in cooking.)

Add the porcini and the soaking wine to the pan and bring everything to a boil. Cover and put in the oven. Cook the Stracotto for about 2 hours, or until you can penetrate the meat with a fork.

Take the meat out, slice it, and set it aside. Add a scoop of tomatoes to the sauce, boil for a few minutes, and then put the meat back in the pot. Let it cook another few minutes and serve it with good bread.

OSSOBUCO AL VINO E TARRAGONE

VEAL SHANK IN WINE AND TARRAGON SAUCE

In Tuscany, we cook any kind of shank—pork, lamb, veal. But I have to be honest. Nothing is as tasty or juicy as the veal shank. And remember the marrow—it's the honey of the dish.

PANTRY	COLD STORAGE	MARKET
All-purpose flour	Garlic, finely chopped	Veal shanks (center cut, about 2 inches thick, 1 per person)
Salt	Carrots, julienned	
Black pepper	Beef, chicken, or vegetable broth	Fresh tarragon
Olive oil		
Red wine (good-quality)		

Preheat the oven to medium-hot. Dust the veal shanks with a bit of flour, salt, and pepper. Cover the bottom of a pan with olive oil, and when it is very hot, add the veal and brown on all sides. Set aside.

In another large ovenproof pan, sauté the garlic and carrots over medium heat in a little olive oil. Add the veal shanks and a couple glasses of wine. Turn up the heat and cook until the liquid is reduced by half. Cover the meat with broth and add tarragon, salt, and pepper to taste.

Cover pan, put in the oven, and cook as long as it takes for the meat to practically fall off the bone, about 1½ hours.

Remove the pan from the oven, take out the veal shanks, and reduce the sauce a bit. Serve the sauce on top of the veal shanks.

VARIATION Cooked Arborio rice that has been added at the last minute is a good addition to the sauce.

A PIG FOR ALL SEASONS

Every year my father would have a contadino *raise and butcher a pig. A huge table would be cleared to prepare the pig, and every part would be used: the blood for blood sausage; the head, ears, and feet for soppressata (an Italian salami); the ribs for spareribs; the loin for chops; the ham for prosciutto. In one or two days the whole animal was transformed, and the pig that we had been keeping in the* contadino's *yard was now being kept in the cellar. We would then have prosciutto in the summer and cotechino in the fall. It was wonderful.*

This is how people do these things in the country and even in the cities of Tuscany. It is impossible to imagine any city person who doesn't have a connection with a contadino *who can supply eggs, mushrooms, and vegetables in season. As much as we can, we like to preserve foods when they are in season, so there will always be something out of season to enjoy all year long.*

During the Middle Ages, people used to preserve meats and vegetables to use in winter and whenever there was war. They would close their doors and protect themselves from starving by living off this huge amount of stored food. They could stay behind those doors forever.

Tuscans still like to protect themselves in this way. You will never find them in their houses without food. Maybe other things will be missing, but if they have to choose between having food or something else, Tuscans will always choose food.

COTECHINO
E LENTICCHIE
PORK SAUSAGE AND LENTILS

entils are thought to bring good luck and prosperity if eaten the last few days of the year, so from Christmas to New Year's, we make lentil salad, served warm or at room temperature. I like it with olive oil, celery, salt and pepper, and just a touch of vinegar. Lentils are also good in soup made with olive oil and wine, with a little bit of vinegar added at the end and some rosemary to sharpen the taste. But the way I like lentils best is with cotechino, pork sausage. This dish can also be made with cannellini beans, for a very traditional Tuscan and Emiglia-Romagna dish.

PANTRY	COLD STORAGE	MARKET
Lentils, soaked overnight and drained		Cotechino (pig's foot) sausage
Olive oil		
Red wine		
Salt		
Black pepper		
Canned tomatoes		

Cook the lentils in enough boiling water to cover until just tender. Drain and set aside. Pierce the sausage with a fork and boil it for as long as it takes to release the grease—about 30 minutes. Then slice it.

Sauté the sliced sausage in olive oil until browned and cooked through. Add the lentils and a splash of wine. Turn the heat up to high and cook until the wine is reduced slightly, then lower the heat and continue to cook for a few more minutes. Season with salt and pepper. Add some tomatoes, cover, and cook until the flavors combine and the dish is hot.

FIRST FIND A FENCE . . .

I'll tell you how we grill in Tuscany. The first thing we do is find a fence. You may think I'm kidding, but I once heard of a bunch of guys picnicking out in the countryside in Maremma who had about fifty pounds of ribs they wanted to grill. It would have taken them all day to cook the ribs on the barbecue they had brought, but they spotted a wrought iron fence in front of a nearby house, took it down, doused it with olive oil, stretched it over the fire, and cooked all the ribs at once. Then they put the fence right back where they found it—cold.

Shepherds dig a hollow in the ground and build a small U-shaped barrier around it with stones. This barrier protects the fire from wind and also keeps the ashes from blowing in their faces. They fill the alcove with dry wood and make a grill of chicken wire.

The brother-in-law of my friend Giancarlo told me he used to go camping with Giancarlo's father. They stayed at a small camp in the middle of nowhere. There wasn't a grill available to cook on, so they used to grill on top of the bedspring. At night, they put the bedspring back, put the mattress on top, and went to sleep. It worked fine.

ROSTINCIANA

GRILLED SPARERIBS

There is a better way to eat spareribs than to smother them in barbecue sauce. Serve them grilled, with a very simple salad of field arugula or warm beans with olive oil.

PANTRY	COLD STORAGE	MARKET
Salt		Pork spareribs
Black pepper		
Olive oil		

Mix some salt, pepper, and olive oil in your hand and rub each rib with the mixture, especially around the edges where the fat is. Grill the spareribs over a hot wood fire, a barbecue, or under the broiler until crisp.

NOTE You can also put the spareribs in a hot oven, in a pan with just enough olive oil to cover the bottom. They will cook almost the same way as if on the grill, but it will take longer. Start checking for tenderness with a fork after about 30 minutes. If you want them crisper, pour off the excess liquid and put the ribs back in the oven until well done.

ROGNONE DI MAIALE

GRILLED PORK KIDNEYS

PANTRY	COLD STORAGE	MARKET
Bay leaves		Pork kidneys
Salt		Fresh sage
Black pepper		Bacon, preferably
Olive oil		pancetta, sliced

Clean the kidneys. On each kidney, place a bay leaf and 1 or 2 sage leaves. Wrap each with the bacon, then sprinkle with salt, pepper, and olive oil. Place kidneys on a hot grill or under the broiler and cook until medium rare. Start checking to see if they are getting firm after about 10 minutes. This is pure honey, but don't eat the bay leaf.

VARIATION This recipe can also be made with veal kidneys. Serve them medium-rare, slightly bloody in the center.

BISTECCA ALLA FIORENTINA

BEEFSTEAK, FLORENTINE STYLE

Tuscany is known everywhere in the world for its Beefsteak Florentine. Actually, if you have to give credit to a province for this steak, the province is Maremma. Let me explain.

In the nineteenth century, Maremma wasn't yet Maremma. It was an area divided into a few huge estates that were owned by aristocratic Florentine families, some of them noble and some of them just rich. At that time the system of transportation wasn't as efficient as it is today, so going from Florence to Grosseto, the main city of Maremma, was a long journey. The people moved around the country in carriages called barocci, *pulled by engines called horses and donkeys.*

Scattered all over the countryside were free-ranging cattle, and often these cattle ate ortica, *a type of poisonous grass. Once the cattle ate this grass their stomachs bloated to enormous sizes. There was no point in calling the veterinarian, because by the time he got there the cattle would be dead. Then the rich landowner took the best parts of the cattle—the ribs, steaks, and loin —and the* contadini *got the head and tail.*

After this happened a few times, the contadini *learned. As soon as the cattle started to bloat, they started the wood fire. They cut up the animal, added olive oil, salt, and pepper—and onto the wood fire went the cow's best parts.*

When the Florentine administrators realized how well the contadini *were preparing steak, they tried preparing it the same way. The Florentines enjoyed it so much that they appropriated this method when they went back to their rich houses in Florence. And that's how Bistecca Fiorentina was born.*

PANTRY	COLD STORAGE	MARKET
Olive oil	Lemon wedges	Steak, from the rib, left on the bone (2 inches thick, about ½ pound per person)
Black pepper		
Salt		

Rub the steak on both sides with olive oil and sprinkle it with pepper. Cook over a hot grill or under the broiler until it is rare to medium-rare. Add salt to taste after the meat has cooked; if you do it before, the salt draws out all the juices from the meat. Serve with lemon wedges.

BISTECCA TAGLIATA ALLA FIORENTINA

SLICED STEAK, FLORENTINE STYLE

In Tuscany we have a special kind of beef cattle called Chianina. It's a breed that goes back to the Romans and makes the best steak in Tuscany. Tuscany is the only region of Italy where people eat meat from the cattle they raise. In the rest of the country the beef comes from Poland, Hungary, Czechoslovakia, and so forth—it's all European beef. The steak in the United States is very good, but the perfect steak is in Tuscany. To prepare it this way, the meat has to be left on the bone, it should weigh at least between a pound and a pound and a half, and it ought to be at least two inches thick.

PANTRY	COLD STORAGE	MARKET
Olive oil (good-quality)		Steak, from the rib and left on the bone (2 or 3 inches thick, about ½ pound per person)
		Fresh rosemary
		Fresh sage

Grill or broil the steak until it is rare, but don't put any olive oil or seasoning on it. Slice the steak and put the slices on a plate.

Meanwhile, in a small frying pan over low heat, heat some olive oil with the rosemary and sage leaves. Keep over low heat long enough for the olive oil to get so hot it creates a lot of smoke and the herbs begin to burn. Immediately pour the oil and herbs over the steak. The herbs will perfume the meat and the hot oil will finish the cooking perfectly. Pour off the excess oil and serve.

THE LAMB SEASON

*E*aster is one of the three holidays when Tuscan families get together no matter how far they have to travel. (The other holidays are Christmas and Ferragosto—the Day of the Assumption, on August 15.)

Easter Sunday begins with a ritual: the benediction of the eggs. People carry hard-boiled eggs, carefully wrapped in napkins, to 8:00 A.M. Mass—one egg for each member of the family. The priest blesses the eggs and then everyone takes them home and eats them with a little salt. Try eating a cold hard-cooked egg first thing in the morning and see how it tastes—Boom!—you've got a stone right in your stomach. It doesn't matter if people are religious or not; everyone starts Easter Sunday this way.

We ate our eggs with a Tuscan Easter breakfast cake that has a very light cheese taste and is made with sesame and anise seeds. The cake has a spicy aroma and is good with black coffee.

It seems that all Tuscan families have their favorite local restaurant for Easter dinner, but my family liked to search out a different one each year. It would take fifteen or twenty minutes to get the whole family into the car, and then we would drive an hour into the countryside. We would have reserved twenty or thirty tables outside in the sun, and everyone would meet there. And there were always a lot of kids, so we made sure there was a playground nearby.

In Tuscany, Easter is an outdoor event—the first outing of spring. It's the celebration of something to come. The trees are full of color, and flowers are everywhere. It smells so good that people like to just lie down on the ground and enjoy the first sun. Who wants to stay inside?

Easter is also the beginning of the picnic season in Tuscany, so even if people don't go to a restaurant, they still eat outside. They find space in a backyard, by the side of the road, wherever they can find room. They put up tables, lay down tablecloths, and set up everything: Easter lamb, lamb with pasta, lamb stew with artichokes, or a combination of all of these. It's a long lunch that starts, maybe, at one or two o'clock in the afternoon and goes on until four or five o'clock. Everybody enjoys it. It's almost as if they feel they have to recuperate from the winter spent indoors. Easter is really a time for rejuvenation, for getting back to a normal outdoor life.

AGNELLO DI PASQUA

EASTER LAMB

In the spring, especially around Easter, Tuscans eat a lot of lamb. They eat it all year long, but the best-quality lamb is available during the Easter season. How do you choose a good lamb? As they say in Maremma, it must be young, tender, and with a pink face. With this dish I like to serve fried baby artichokes (page 208), which are just coming into season at this time. This is a beautiful Easter lunch: roast baby lamb, roasted potatoes, and deep-fried baby artichokes with fresh mint leaves.

PANTRY	COLD STORAGE	MARKET
Olive oil	Garlic, slivered	Fresh rosemary
Salt	Potatoes (optional)	Leg of lamb or whole spring baby lamb for a large party
Black pepper		

Coat the bottom and sides of a roasting pan with olive oil. With the tip of a sharp knife, make small gashes all over the lamb and stuff with rosemary leaves and slivers of garlic. Coat the lamb with olive oil and a dusting of salt and pepper. If you want, put potatoes all around the lamb; season them also with rosemary, salt, pepper, and olive oil.

Roast the lamb in a very slow oven until the skin is crisp and the roast releases liquid when pierced with a fork. The only thing you have to do once in awhile is add some water if you see the meat getting dry. Allow about 30 minutes per pound cooking time for medium-done lamb. If the lamb is cooked a little less or a little more, it won't spoil your meal, and it won't spoil your Easter.

SPEZZATINO DI AGNELLO E CARCIOFI

LAMB AND ARTICHOKE STEW

For this dish, use the smallest artichokes you can find and meat from the leg that is usually used for stews. The stew can be cooked on top of the stove or in the oven.

PANTRY	COLD STORAGE	MARKET
Olive oil	Lemon juice	Artichokes
White wine	Garlic, smashed	Fresh mint
	Beef or chicken broth (optional)	Lamb, from the leg, cubed

If you are using the oven, preheat it to medium. Remove the outside leaves of the artichokes and cut the tented inside part into quarters. Put them immediately into a bowl of water that you have made acidic with some lemon juice. Set them aside.

Cover the bottom of a large ovenproof pot with olive oil and add the garlic, mint leaves, and lamb. Brown the lamb over high heat, then add 2 or 3 generous splashes of wine. (Don't use a cheap wine; it really changes the taste of the sauce.) Once the wine has evaporated a bit, remove the lamb, skim off the fat, and put the artichokes into the pot.

Let the artichokes cook for a bit and acquire the taste of the sauce, then put the lamb back in the pot, cover it, and place it in the oven. Start to check the lamb and the artichokes after about 30 minutes to see if they're tender when pierced with a fork. You can also cook the dish on top of the stove over medium heat. If the stew gets too dry, add some water; the lamb doesn't have to be floating in liquid, but it just shouldn't dry out.

SPEZZATINO DI AGNELLO E PEPERONI

LAMB AND SWEET PEPPER STEW

*U*se yellow and red bell peppers in this stew because they are sweeter. A leg of lamb is the preferred cut of meat here because it is very meaty and simple to trim and cut in pieces.

PANTRY	COLD STORAGE	MARKET
Olive oil	Garlic	Red peppers
Salt		Yellow peppers
Black pepper		Lamb pieces
White wine		

Cut the peppers lengthwise into slices. Rinse them in cold water and drain well. Set them aside.

Put the olive oil, garlic, and lamb pieces in a large pot. Brown the lamb over a hot fire, add salt and pepper to taste, then add two or three good splashes of wine. (Don't use a cheap wine—it will change the taste of the sauce.) Once the wine has evaporated a bit, add the peppers. Let them cook for a while and acquire the taste of the sauce, then add a little more wine so that the stew stays moist. Cover the pot and put it in a moderate oven until the lamb and the peppers are cooked. You can also cook the whole dish on top of the stove over medium heat—not too high. If the stew gets too dry, add some water. The lamb doesn't have to be floating in liquid, it just shouldn't dry out.

IL POLLAME

BIRDS
OF
A
FEATHER

At one time in the south of Tuscany, there were many bandits. Tuscans call these bandits briganti. *They were so fierce that they smoked cigars with the lit end in their mouths so that soldiers or enemies searching for them in the woods at night wouldn't see the glow from their cigars. Briganti is a great word, more romantic than "bandit."*

The brigante *is a lonely man with some kind of principle or idea behind him. He isn't a thief just because he's bored or lazy. For example, there was a bandit called "Paro e Disparo." Despite his criminal record, which was pages and pages and pages long, this man remained completely free with the help of the* contadini *who loved and protected him. He was doing nice things for them; he robbed the rich and gave to the poor. Finally one night he was arrested. When the officials tried to find out how many other members were in this wild bunch of bandits, Paro e Disparo gave an answer that was typically Tuscan and very poetic: "We're an odd number and no more than one." The next day he was hanged as an example to the people.*

One day I was in a tiny restaurant in the hills near Capalbio, and I noticed that all the pictures on the wall were photographs of bandits who had overrun Maremma many years ago. (I loved hearing stories about them when I was a child.) I asked the owner why he had collected these photos, and he answered in a very heavy Orbetello accent, "They remind me of where I belong. I grew up here and my family is from here. We don't know anything south of Rome or north of Florence, and most of the time we don't give a damn. Usually when people talk about where they come from, they brag about some literary person, or a priest, or an archbishop who is from their village and who represents it in a nice way. Unfortunately, I come from a village with the biggest criminal the country ever had, and we took him for what he is."

When my meal was finally brought to the table, the chicken was done in a very strange way. Even though it's a local dish, I'd never seen it before. It was called pollo scappato alla tiburzi—*"chicken escaped, Tiburzi style." I asked the owner to explain the name, and he told me that it's the kind of chicken you end up with when you've got the police on your tail; you're hiding in the woods, you run when you hear them coming, and when you come back your chicken is burnt. The only thing you can put on it to save the taste is lemon juice.*

Those are the stories that make me think very fondly about my country.

Page 196: **The Cook by Zanobi Strozzi**

POLLO AL LIMONE
CHICKEN WITH LEMON

PANTRY	COLD STORAGE	MARKET
Olive oil	Garlic, sliced	Rosemary (fresh, if available)
Salt	Lemon juice	Chicken, cut up
Black pepper		

Preheat the oven to medium. Mix a little olive oil, salt, pepper, rosemary, garlic, and lots of lemon juice in a large bowl. Marinate the chicken for 2 or 3 hours, turning occasionally in the marinade.

Remove the chicken from the marinade, put it in a baking dish, and put it in the oven. Cook chicken slowly until it's tender and the juices run clear, turning the chicken several times. Check for doneness in about 45 minutes. When it's tender, run it under a hot broiler to give it some more color.

POLLO ALLA CACCIATORA
CHICKEN, HUNTER'S STYLE

PANTRY	COLD STORAGE	MARKET
White wine	Garlic, smashed	Chicken, cut up
Salt		Rosemary (fresh, if available)
Black pepper		Fresh thyme
Dried porcini (optional)		Fresh sage
Canned tomatoes		

Preheat the oven to medium. Put the chicken in an ovenproof pan with garlic, rosemary, thyme, sage, and enough wine to cover. Sprinkle with salt and pepper and let marinate for at least 1 hour. If you use dried porcini, soak them in the same marinade, then drain and add to chicken.

Place pan over high heat and cook, turning the chicken once in awhile until it gains some color and the wine cooks down. Then add tomatoes, cover, and put the pan in the oven. Cook until chicken is tender; check for doneness in about an hour. Add a bit of water if the mixture gets too dry. Serve with the sauce and some crusty bread.

POLLETTO ALLA DIAVOLA

DEVIL-STYLE FREE-RANGE CHICKEN

The most amazing thing about chickens is that they make eggs. I used to watch them for hours, hoping to catch them at it, but I never once saw a chicken lay an egg—never. Eggs are the only interesting thing about chickens, until you start to think about cooking them.

Pollo ruspante is the kind of free-range chicken that people can only dream about today—so meaty and tender and tasty. They are raised in a way that disappeared a long time ago. In older times in Tuscany, chickens were fed with corn, yes, but also with leftover pasta or lunch from the day before, mixed with vegetable broth or minestrone verdura, *or any other food from the house. We called these chickens "ruspante" because a* ruspante *is the one that scratches in the dirt to find food.*

This chicken dish is made with a two- or three-week-old free-range chicken, which is turning up everywhere in the American markets. Basically, these chickens are left free to grow in open spaces, and they just eat, eat, eat for two or three weeks. This gives their meat a better quality, with less fat, and the skin is excellent. The chicken can be baked or broiled. Have the butcher butterfly the chicken and break the ribs so the bird is very flat.

PANTRY	COLD STORAGE	MARKET
Crushed red pepper	Lemon wedges	Free-range chicken
Salt		
Olive oil		

If you are baking the chicken, preheat the oven to hot. Then put some red pepper on your hand and rub it on the skin and on the cavity side. Do the same thing with salt and then with olive oil until chicken is moist. Put the chicken, skin side down, on a hot grill or broiler or in the oven to bake. Cook about 15 minutes, turn, and cook about 15 minutes on the other side.

The chicken is done when it is crisp on the outside and firm but not dry on the inside. When you serve it, just sprinkle the chicken with a little bit of olive oil and serve with a wedge of lemon.

PETTI DI POLLO AL FUNGHETTO

STUFFED BREASTS OF CHICKEN WITH MUSHROOM SAUCE

PANTRY	COLD STORAGE	MARKET
All-purpose flour	Milk	Eggs, separated (2 yolks to 1 white)
Salt	Butter	Boneless whole breasts of chicken
Black pepper		Prosciutto, thinly sliced
Olive oil		Smoked mozzarella, sliced
White wine		Fresh mushrooms, sliced
Canned tomatoes		Fresh rosemary

Whip the egg yolks and whites and mix in a bowl with a bit of flour, salt and pepper, and a splash of milk. Set aside.

Pound the chicken breasts until flattened. Place a slice of prosciutto and a slice of smoked mozzarella on top of each breast and fold over so that the meat and cheese are enclosed inside. Pinch the edges together, dip in the egg mixture, and allow excess egg to drip off the chicken.

Heat olive oil in a frying pan and sauté the chicken over high heat on both sides until golden; the egg *pastella* will seal the chicken. Use fresh olive oil to cook each additional chicken breast.

To make the sauce, melt butter in a pan and add the mushrooms, rosemary, enough wine to moisten the mushrooms, and salt and pepper. Cook a couple of minutes over high heat, then add the chicken breasts. Lower the heat to medium and cover the mixture with equal amounts of tomatoes and wine. Cover the pan and check for doneness in 15 or 20 minutes.

NEW YEAR'S EVE

My mother and father spend days preparing the food for New Year's Eve. At least twenty people come to our house. I love the menu. The appetizer always includes eel, the huge eel called capitone. It is cleaned, cut into pieces, and stewed very slowly with a bit of rosemary, marjoram, white wine, and tomatoes. This is usually served with a plate of prosciutto and crostini, raw vegetables, or artichokes preserved in olive oil.

The second course is a cup of broth. The broth is very important; it is traditional at any holiday meal in Italy and always follows the appetizer.

Then comes the pasta. My mother makes a beautiful lasagne of six or seven layers filled with ricotta, cinnamon, and nutmeg. The meat sauce is made of veal, game, and poultry—all ground together and browned in the classic way with odori, garlic, and good red wine. It cooks for a long time, and as it cooks you can smell the scent of nutmeg all over the house.

The third course is always capon stuffed with sausage and chestnuts, a traditional New Year's dish. There are many ways of making the stuffing; some are sweeter, some moister, but Mother's has the most earthy taste (see recipe on opposite page).

After the meal we have tortelloni dolci for dessert: pockets of dough stuffed with ricotta and a type of Italian crème de cassis. The tortelloni require lots of preparation, and it takes my mother about a day and a half to make enough for all of us. She is forced to make two or three hundred, because when you start eating tortelloni, it's hard to stop.

As a kid I could hardly wait for the dessert because it always included a practical joke. My mother never stuffs all of the tortelloni with ricotta; she always fills some of them with something we call stoppa, which is like straw and sticks to your mouth.

One time my grandfather bit into one of the stoppa tortelloni. I was looking around to see who would get one, so I remember how he looked when he ate it: stuck and disgusted. He got so mad he left the house and didn't see my mother for two months.

CAPPONE AL FORNO
ROASTED STUFFED CAPON

I prepare capon many different ways. Sometimes I just make a simple broth using capon, carrots, celery, and onions, and it's one of the best broths in the world. I serve it with tortellini, tagliolini, and other pastas. But my favorite way to fix capon is stuffed with chestnuts and sausage. The same stuffing can be used with turkey or chicken, but I like it best with capon.

PANTRY	COLD STORAGE	MARKET
Red wine	Butter	Capon, with interiors
Salt		Fresh chestnuts
Black pepper		Fennel seeds
		Sweet Italian sausage
		Fresh sage

Preheat the oven to medium. Rub the inside of the capon with butter. Place chestnuts in a pot of water and add fennel seeds and red wine for flavor. Boil until the chestnuts are done—when they can be penetrated with a fork. Start checking them after about 10 minutes, because you don't want them to get too soft. Let the chestnuts cook, then peel and cut them into pieces.

Remove the skin from the sausage and cut it into sections. Place the sausage in a pan and, as it cooks, break it into small pieces. Season with salt and pepper. When the sausage is done, remove it to a bowl, leaving the grease behind.

Sauté the interiors in butter and sage until cooked, then chop them. Add the interiors and chestnuts to the sausage and mix well. Stuff this mixture inside the capon, place capon in the oven, and roast for about 1 hour per pound. If you see that the capon is getting too dry as it cooks, add water.

VARIATION This capon is also good stuffed with Polenta (page 87) and sausage.

I VEGETALI E LE INSALATE

VEGETABLES

AND

SALADS

At the turn of the century, when my grandmother was still a little girl, she attended a huge wedding in Maremma. At least three hundred people from the region were invited because the bride was the only daughter of one of the richest farmers in Maremma. After the ceremony at the church, everyone continued the celebration at the farm, the bride and groom leading the procession in a carriage and the others following on horses, donkeys, and bicycles.

Long tables had been set up in the courtyard in front of the house, but they soon spilled out onto the surrounding land as the guests increased in number. This always happens in Tuscany.

The tables displayed a variety of vegetables—what my grandfather called "the appetizers of the proletariat." There were huge baskets of fresh green fava beans, fried artichokes ready to be dipped into olive oil and salt, celery sticks and carrots, and large bowls of panzanella, the ubiquitous Tuscan bread salad. Kids passed rough wooden trays filled with fettunta and grilled broccoli rabe. But this was only to whet the appetite; the serious cooking was yet to begin.

Can you imagine cooking for three hundred? They did it by having each family prepare its own specialty for the entire group. Different dishes were cooked in every

part of the yard. The Cecchi roasted pigs on spits; the Nencini prepared crostini and sausage; the Buzzatti grilled vegetables, and so on. And all the while, the women and children brushed the food with branches of rosemary dipped in olive oil.

The Nardini family was in charge of game. They cooked a huge deer, the cervo, that we have in Tuscany. Because they liked the strong, gamy taste, they didn't marinate it as we do today; they simply tenderized the meat by pounding it to break the fibers. They pierced the meat, stuffed prosciutto and sage in the holes,

brushed it with olive oil, and let it roast. The unusual part came at the end, when they covered the venison with tendrils from grapevines. The curly parts at the end of the vines, which grow again the following year, have a strong acidic taste—much stronger than the grapes themselves—and act like alcohol to tenderize the meat.

Since my great-grandfather was a fisherman, our family was in charge of the seafood. They grilled eel and striped bass (branzino). They butterflied the mullet (cefalo), cut fresh tomatoes in chunks, and squeezed them over the top with a dash of salt, hot pepper, and olive oil. My family still makes this dish.

My grandmother described the wedding as an orgy of sights and smells. You know what eels smell like

the cooking chicken livers added a gamy, pungent odor, but I'm sure the dominant aromas were wine and vinegar and rosemary.

The only dessert they had was fruit, except for the wedding cake.

Open spaces and courtyards are still traditional places for weddings in the Tuscan countryside, and vegetables still introduce the meals, maybe because so many Tuscans marry in the spring or summer. But now the barbecues and skewers have been replaced with vans parked out in the courtyard, bearing the name of a local catering company.

when they are grilled? So strong and aromatic you can almost feel the sea and taste the salt. The pigs were very sweet and aromatic also, because they were cooked with bay laurel. The stewing wild boar and

The wedding party of a friend of my grandmother's

BROCCOLETTI SALTATI
SAUTÉED BROCCOLI RABE

PANTRY	COLD STORAGE	MARKET
Olive oil	Garlic, smashed	Broccoli rabe
Crushed red pepper		
Salt		

Cut the long stems off the vegetable, leaving the leaves and flowers. Wash the broccoli rabe well in a lot of cold water, but do not dry it.

Put the garlic, about 2 cloves per person, in the bottom of a deep pan with enough olive oil just to cover the bottom. Turn the heat up high and when the oil is so hot that you can see the fumes from the oil, stand back and toss in the drained broccoli rabe, being careful that the oil doesn't splash. Add the red pepper and salt to taste, toss, and cook only long enough to wilt the leaves. Serve immediately, as an appetizer or with sausage or any red meat.

CARCIOFI ALLA GIUDEA
FRIED BABY ARTICHOKES

PANTRY	COLD STORAGE	MARKET
Olive oil	Lemon juice (optional)	Baby artichokes, cleaned
Salt	Garlic, finely chopped	
Black pepper		Fresh mint, chopped

Take the tough outer leaves and stems off the artichokes. Cut off the prickly tops of the remaining leaves and soak each one in water and lemon juice so they don't turn black as you work. When finished, take them out of the water and, with the heel of your hand, press down on each artichoke so the leaves loosen and separate a bit.

Fill a large pan with enough olive oil to let the artichokes float. Set over high heat until the oil gets very hot and smoky. Put all the artichokes in at one time and fry until they are brown and crispy. They should come out crunchy on the outside and tender and juicy inside.

When cooked, put them in a bowl with the olive oil clinging to the leaves. Add garlic, salt, pepper, and mint. Mix and add lemon juice.

VEGETALI ALLA GRIGLIA

GRILLED VEGETABLES

My grandmother uses nettles in the fire when grilling vegetables because this plant acts as a good filter between the vegetables and the flame. It keeps the vegetables from burning and makes them smell good. I've always thought that nettles were the nastiest plant. When I was twelve, I hid in a field with my girlfriend. My first kiss, and I finished with a face full of nettles. It almost changed my mind about romance!

Anyway, this is how we grill over a wood fire in Tuscany. Lay dry wood on the bottom of a grill. Place green wood on top of the dry wood. (The green wood doesn't burn, but it creates aromatic smoke.) Brush sprigs of fresh herbs with olive oil, lay them between layers of folded chicken wire, and put this on top of the green wood. On top of the chicken wire, place vegetables brushed with olive oil. Grill until you have something that tastes and smells good.

I've started to grill many vegetables I once thought couldn't be cooked this way and, believe me, it's an undiscovered world. If vegetables are exposed to the fire for a very short time, there is a natural reaction that makes them taste great. I've tried grilling everything, even fiddlehead ferns. They taste great, steamed first and then grilled.

Grilled vegetables can be served with prosciutto or salami and are especially good with Fettunta (page 43). A large platter of assorted grilled vegetables is an excellent appetizer. Use whatever is available, season by season.

PANTRY	COLD STORAGE	MARKET
Salt		Any combination of fresh vegetables
Black pepper		
Olive oil		

Place vegetables on a flat pan (a pizza pan works perfectly) and season with salt, pepper, and olive oil. Place under the broiler, over a wood fire, or even in a hot oven. Turn once while they cook.

Any way you cook them, these vegetables come out perfectly—moist and tasty. Of course, they are crunchier if you put them over a wood fire or under the broiler, but if that's not possible, the oven is not the worst solution. Sprinkle with lemon juice or vinegar if you like.

SALAD GREENS

WILD GREENS There are some kinds of wild salad greens that grow only in Tuscany as far as I know. They grow everywhere, as do the herbs. Once you know them, you can find them in the fields there. They are also served in restaurants in the spring and fall. The varieties I like most are *mesticanza* (lamb's quarters) and *rughetta* (wild chicory). *Rughetta* is excellent alone or with tomatoes and a simple dressing of olive oil and lemon. *Mesticanza* grows on sandy beaches near pine woods. It has hairy, thick leaves, very long and narrow. You can't eat it alone; it has to be mixed with something else like wild rugola or wild radicchio, but just a small number of the leaves mixed with any other kind of green gives a salad a better taste, texture, and quality.

People think that salad greens only grow out of the ground, but some greens grow spontaneously in all kinds of places. I have seen the women of Montalcino digging with spoons for the greens that grow in the cracks of the medieval walls surrounding their village. The salad they make is the result of their knowledge of local greens, and they blend these greens in a harmonious combination, always adding the surprising, pungent taste of herbs.

CULTIVATED GREENS There are many varieties of cultivated greens, but most of them are good only for the cows. Romaine? When you finish a salad of that you get up from the table and . . . *Moo!*

FAVORITE SALADS The foundation of most of my salads is rugola. That's the most prestigious salad green in Italy and the one that complements many other greens. The salads I make most often are:

- rugola and tomatoes, with a dressing of vinegar, olive oil, salt, and pepper
- rugola and thin strips of fennel, with a dressing of lemon, olive oil, salt, and pepper
- rugola by itself, with a dressing of vinegar or lemon, olive oil, salt, and pepper
- rugola, Belgian endive, and radicchio with a red wine vinegar dressing

CONDIMENTO PER INSALATA

SALAD DRESSING

If you don't want to kill the taste of the greens, pay attention to the dressing. I make my dressing in the peasant style, with red wine vinegar, olive oil, salt, and pepper. I prepare a goodly amount of dressing in advance and store it in bottles in the refrigerator. The dressing tastes sharper when used with rugola and endive because these greens bring out the sharp taste of the vinegar. Even if you don't refrigerate it, let the oil and vinegar sit awhile in the bottle with some salt, which helps to bind them together.

It's hard to get a mixture of tastes if you pour the oil and vinegar separately because in certain parts of the salad the oil prevails and in other parts the vinegar prevails. If you keep the bottle refrigerated and shake it up when you take it out, the dressing becomes creamy and foamy.

PANTRY	COLD STORAGE	MARKET
Red wine vinegar (good-quality)		
Salt		
Black pepper		
Olive oil		

Use about 1 part vinegar to 3 parts olive oil for a sharp taste. Put vinegar in the bottom of a clean wine bottle or jar. Add salt and pepper, and pour the olive oil on top. Shake well. Taste for seasoning before you splash the dressing on a salad. This is my fancy dressing: vinegar, olive oil, salt, pepper, and nothing else.

PRELUDE TO SPRING

As soon as spring was on its way, my mother would rub her hands together and say, "Finally, it's time for a good spring cleaning." She would put away all the heavy woolen blankets and sweaters. Then she would open all the windows and let out the winter feelings that had been in the house for so many months.

I always identify the springtime with bed mattresses. Our mattresses were entirely handmade, of wool, and all winter we slept in a closed house, pressing down the mattresses on one side. By spring, it was time to freshen the wool. That's when my mother would make an appointment with the materassai—the people who came every year to air out the mattresses for our family.

The materassai brought the mattresses downstairs and put them outside on a huge rug. Then they took out the stitches and opened each mattress—just butterflied it. With a machine they brought with them, they shredded the wool, pulling and stretching it until it was as fluffy and tender and soft as it had been when it was new. Then they stored the stuffing in huge cotton bags while they had their lunch.

The materassai brought all their food with them except their salad. This they picked from the fields which surrounded our house. They knew that they could find tiny field rugola, aromatic herbs, and wild spinach, so they always brought a wine bottle filled with salad dressing. They set up a small table outside, put on it a long loaf of bread, a flask of wine, glasses, and a frittata di pasta that they brought with them. They'd take their time over a good glass of wine, eat their meal, and smoke a cigarette. After lunch they put all the wool inside each mattress cover and, starting with one corner, they would sew them up again.

By sundown, they called to my mother, "Signora Luongo, è finito." And we would have fresh mattresses for the spring and summer. It was like that every year.

PUNTARELLE IN SALSA DI ALICI

PUNTARELLE SALAD WITH ANCHOVY DRESSING

This is not a completely Tuscan dish. It's found near the southern border between Rome and Tuscany. It's a between-borders dish that the Romans think they own.

Puntarelle is a kind of wild chicory that has very long, narrow leaves. It can be found in Italian vegetable markets in the winter until spring.

PANTRY	COLD STORAGE	MARKET
Anchovies	Garlic	Puntarelle
Black pepper		
Red wine vinegar		
Olive oil		

Use all of the puntarelle—the leaves and the heart. Slice the heart lengthwise in very narrow pieces, then soak in ice water until leaves become curly.

To make the dressing, smash together the garlic and the anchovies with a little pepper and enough vinegar to cover the anchovies. (Use plenty of anchovies and garlic if you want a strong taste of these. If you don't like either one, stay away from this recipe.) Now add an equal amount of olive oil and beat well until you have a thick infusion and the oil and vinegar are no longer separated. Put the dressing in the bottom of a salad bowl, add the puntarelle, and mix. Serve with lots of bread on the side to dip into the dressing.

RADICCHIO ROSSO ALL'ARANCIA
RADICCHIO GARNISHED AND SCENTED WITH ORANGES

PANTRY	COLD STORAGE	MARKET
Olive oil	Fresh parsley, chopped (optional)	Orange juice
Red wine vinegar		Lillet apéritif
Salt		Radicchio
Black pepper		Oranges, sliced

Make a dressing of the oil and vinegar and add orange juice and Lillet to taste. Season with salt and pepper.

Place whole radicchio leaves on a chilled plate, top with a slice of orange, and drizzle with the dressing. Sprinkle with parsley, if you wish.

SEGATO DI CARCIOFI CON CAROTE
SALAD OF ARTICHOKES AND CARROTS

PANTRY	COLD STORAGE	MARKET
Anchovies	Lemon, juice and wedges	Artichokes
Red wine vinegar		Salad greens of choice
Olive oil	Carrots, shredded	
Salt	Garlic, chopped	
Black pepper		

Have ready a bowl of water to which you have added some lemon juice. Peel leaves off artichokes almost to the heart, then thinly slice the artichokes lengthwise and quickly toss the slices into the acidulated water before they turn color. Shred the carrots and set aside.

To make the dressing, mash the anchovies into the vinegar, add the garlic, and stir in the oil. I use 1 part vinegar to 3 parts oil. Season with salt and pepper. (Go easy on the salt because of the anchovies.)

To assemble the salad, place the greens on a chilled plate, put the drained artichokes on the greens, and top with the carrots. Drizzle dressing over all and serve with lemon wedges.

PANZANELLA

BREAD SALAD

*P*anzanella is one more example of the many ways Tuscan cooks use bread. In this recipe, the bread captures the sharp essence of the dressing and contrasts perfectly with the fresh, crisp vegetables of the salad.

PANTRY	COLD STORAGE	MARKET
Red wine vinegar	Vegetable broth	Day-old bread, chunked
Olive oil	Red onion, thinly sliced	Cucumber, peeled and thinly sliced
Salt		Scallions (white part), thinly sliced
Black pepper		Fresh tomatoes, chunked

Moisten the bread with cool broth and squeeze out excess liquid. Place the bread in a bowl and sprinkle with vinegar. Mix well so the bread has a chance to absorb the flavor. Put cucumbers, scallions, onion, and tomatoes in the bowl with the bread. Add olive oil, salt, and pepper to taste, if needed. Add more vinegar and oil to taste, also if needed. Refrigerate before serving. This salad can also be kept in the refrigerator and served the next day.

I DOLCI

THE
PERFECT
ENDING

Food isn't the whole story. The environment and the company you're with are as important as what you're eating. My restaurant is like my house—a private place that I happen to share with other people. I want people to feel comfortable; to be able to share with me those moments when everything comes together. Here is what I would imagine to be the perfect ending to a great meal at my restaurant: one day, people at one table will start talking to people at another table, even though they've never seen each other before. Someone will turn a chair around and say, "Oh, do you want to play cards with us?" Then I can put their two tables together, as we do at the trattorias in Tuscany. And why not? It would be like having a little bit of Tuscany in my restaurant. The power of the imagination is the only thing that's worthwhile.

As far back as my memory can go, all the beautiful meals I have had in Tuscany with my family and friends end with a platter of cheese, a bowl of fruit, and perhaps a glass of Vin Santo.

The cheese was usually the sheep's milk cheese caciotta, and there was fresh ricotta or maybe some cheeses like stracchino or taleggio from other regions. But most of all it was caciotta, fresh or aged, and a good glass of wine.

In Tuscany, the major cheeses are made from sheep's milk, which gets harder and sharper as it ages. When it's fresh, up to four or five weeks, it's called caciotta di pecora, or fresh pecorino. Longer than eight weeks, it's called pecorino stagionato.

Even though all caciotta is made from sheep's milk, the taste varies from town to town and from area to area. The local differences have to do with the diets of the sheep and the individual techniques handed down from father to son. When you travel around Tuscany, if you ask for caciotta or pecorino, you will be happily surprised because they all taste different.

Caciotta reminds me of my godfather, who is a painter in Florence. He uses cheese to clean his mouth after meals. He says it's better than toothpaste. He takes a bite of cheese and a swallow of wine, and swishes the whole thing around in his mouth before chewing the cheese and swallowing it. He does this after every meal to get ready for the next meal.

Another type of cheese made from sheep's milk or cow's milk is fresh ricotta, which is a very creamy, light cheese. Sometimes it's served on a slice of bread with black pepper and just a little bit of olive oil sprinkled on top. I grew up with ricotta served in the morning on a piece of toasted bread, with black coffee, or with sugar sprinkled on top at five in the afternoon, for what we call merenda. Tuscans may produce a limited quantity of cheeses, but they are unlimited in quality.

If there is one thing that all kitchen tables of Tuscany have in common, it is a nice bowl of fruit, which changes its colors with the seasons. In May we look forward to seeing the lively red of cherries; later in the summer, it's the velvet yellow and pink of peaches alongside the shy green of pears. With the fall comes the deep golden, thick, juicy color of oranges and tangerines mixed with the woody brown of almonds, walnuts, and chestnuts in their shells. They're always on the table, accessible to any member of the family or guest who passes by. In certain country houses a platter of cheese under a glass bell may be on the table with the fruit.

Maybe more than in many other parts of Italy and other parts of the world, Tuscans like to end the meal with a nice apple or pear and cheese. There is a saying in Tuscany, "Never let the peasant hear how good is the cheese with the pear." It's one of the best combinations—the sweet taste of pear and the fresh, milky taste of cheese.

Maybe the coat of arms of the Tuscan dessert should be a silhouette of a bottle of Vin Santo next to a few Prato cookies. Vin Santo was known during the time of the Medici family, and it was served as a dessert wine in the most aristocratic families, always with the Pratesi cookies. These are the "sweet tooth" of Tuscany, the most popular dessert. But even without the cookies, the wine has a great life of its own.

Vin Santo is made from Muscat grapes and used to be the wine associated with the monasteries. Many reasons have been given for why it's been called Vin Santo, or holy wine, but when I was a kid my father told me about the monks who used to travel from door to door throughout Tuscany to bring charitable assistance to the sick and elderly, always offering a little shot of this mysterious sweet wine. Since it had the power to give a little relief to suffering and loneliness, the wine became known among the peasants as Vin Santo.

My Socialist uncle, however, says the name Vin Santo had nothing to do with charity. It was produced by the monks and nuns as a form of revenue and, last but not least, for their own pleasure. I'll settle for not knowing where this name comes from. I don't want to disappoint either my uncle or my father.

FRAGOLE ALL'ACETO

STRAWBERRIES IN VINEGAR

I always wash strawberries in white wine. If I use water, the strawberries lose some of their taste, but wine helps them maintain a sweet, sparkling flavor. The wine doesn't have to be expensive.

In Tuscany, we use red wine vinegar for this recipe, but you can vary the taste by substituting raspberry or strawberry vinegar. If you don't like vinegar, stay away from this recipe. It definitely has a vinegary taste, though when the dish is chilled, the vinegar loses its bite.

PANTRY	COLD STORAGE	MARKET
White wine		Wild or cultivated fresh strawberries
Red wine vinegar, or raspberry or strawberry vinegar		
Sugar		

Rinse the strawberries in white wine. If you are using cultivated strawberries, remove the hulls; if they are wild, leave them on. Drain the berries, place them in a shallow bowl, and sprinkle with vinegar and a bit of sugar. If you are using raspberry or strawberry vinegar, use much less sugar than if you are using red wine vinegar (or you may not want to use any sugar at all). Chill for 30 minutes, then serve.

PESCHE AL VINO ROSSO

PEACHES IN RED WINE

PANTRY	COLD STORAGE	MARKET
Red wine (good-quality)		Very ripe, fresh peaches

Wash and slice the peaches, but don't peel them. Put the slices in a bowl and cover them with a young red wine. Refrigerate for 1 hour, then serve chilled.

FICHI SECCHI E NOCI

DRIED FIGS AND WALNUTS

T*his is a perfect treat for winter nights, especially around the Christmas holidays. Use dried figs of the best quality, not extremely dried out and not extremely hard.*

PANTRY	COLD STORAGE	MARKET
Walnuts, shelled		Dried figs
Vin Santo		

With a sharp knife, slice the figs almost in half horizontally. Stuff a shelled walnut into the middle of each fig and close it, using some pressure so the figs stay closed. Place figs in a shallow bowl, pour some Vin Santo over them, and let them soak for at least an hour before serving.

MACEDONIA
FRUIT SALAD

M*acedonia can be made of any and all seasonal fruits—apples, pears, bananas, peaches, strawberries, blueberries, raspberries, cherries, watermelon, cantaloupe, honeydew melon, grapes, or oranges. You can even use fresh fruit that is becoming a bit overripe. My favorite version is made with watermelon, cantaloupe, honeydew melon, raisins, and pignolis, mixed with a very little lemon juice—nothing else.*

PANTRY	COLD STORAGE	MARKET
Walnuts, almonds, or pignolis or a combination of nuts	Fresh lemon juice	Seasonal fruit, in any combination
Raisins (optional)		
Sugar		

Wash the fruit, cut it into pieces, and add nuts and raisins, if you are using them. Add lemon juice to taste and a very, very little bit of sugar—just enough to accentuate the natural sweetness of the fruit. Chill for 1 hour, then serve.

INSALATA DI ARANCI
ORANGE SALAD

T*here is a salad made with sliced oranges, good green olive oil, and coarsely ground black pepper that is often served as a dessert or appetizer. It came to mind one day in January when I was in the north in Abetone and it was freezing.*

I was working as an actor and my troupe was hired to perform in a small, simple theater. Very primitive. Wood-burning stoves warmed the audience, and the smell of smoke was everywhere. From the window of my dressing room I could see children skating on the ice. Just before the play began, some of the actors put an orange peel on top of the stove. The smell! It was so strong I could smell it when I went on stage. The warmth from the stove and the smell of the orange made me think of things you can have in the summer.

PANTRY	COLD STORAGE	MARKET
Olive oil		Oranges
Black pepper		

Peel and slice each orange. Sprinkle with olive oil and dust with pepper. Serve this as an appetizer or dessert.

PERE O MELE COTTE

BAKED PEARS OR APPLES

This is a good dessert to serve when the cool months are coming, the trees are losing their leaves, and you want something warm at the end of a meal. Once considered a dish for sick or weak people, these baked fruits are once again finding their place on Tuscan tables. They're quick to make and easy, too.

PANTRY	COLD STORAGE	MARKET
White wine		Large Williams, Comice, or Kiefer pears or large Golden Delicious apples
Sugar		

Preheat the oven to medium. Wash the fruit and place in a baking dish. Mix a bit of water into the wine and use to moisten the fruit. Sprinkle fruit with a little sugar, then bake in the oven until tender. Check for doneness after about 20 minutes.

PESCHE CON NOCI AL FORNO

BAKED PEACHES STUFFED WITH WALNUTS AND CHOCOLATE

PANTRY	COLD STORAGE	MARKET
Sugar		Large firm peaches
Walnuts, shelled and chopped		Baker's sweet chocolate

Preheat the oven to medium. Heat equal amounts of water and sugar over low heat until the sugar is melted. Set aside.

Cutting through the top, remove the pit from each peach, leaving a cavity for stuffing. Set them aside.

Melt the chocolate in the top of a double boiler until it is just melted but not runny. Stir in the walnuts. Fill the cavities of the peaches with this mixture, then wet the top of each peach with a spoonful of the sugar syrup. Bake in the oven until peaches are tender. Check for doneness after 15 minutes.

CASTAGNE ARROSTO

ROASTED CHESTNUTS

In Tuscany, we have so many chestnuts that kids use them instead of stones when they play. For this recipe, Tuscans use the largest chestnuts, the ones we call marroni. You can roast the chestnuts over a fire in a traditional chestnut roasting pan, or if you prefer, you can roast them in the oven in a shallow pan.

PANTRY	COLD STORAGE	MARKET
Sugar		Chestnuts
Salt		
Red wine		

If you plan to bake the chestnuts, preheat the oven to very hot, 400°F.

Make an incision in the flat side of each chestnut. Roast the chestnuts over a fire or in the oven for 10 minutes, then remove from the heat and sprinkle with a little sugar, a little salt, and some red wine. Put them back over the heat to finish roasting. They are cooked once the incisions start to spread open and the nut meats start to pop out of the shells.

Serve with a glass of good red wine.

LA POLENTA DOLCE

SWEET POLENTA

This is a seasonal dessert that people make in the fall until Christmas, because that is when chestnuts are in season and chestnut flour is at its sweetest and freshest. Chestnut flour is available in many Italian specialty markets and sophisticated natural foods stores. It's worth looking for the flour because of the simplicity and exquisite taste of this dessert. If it doesn't come out right the first time, persist. It's worth it to have this for a winter dessert with friends.

PANTRY	COLD STORAGE	MARKET
Salt		Bottled spring water
Sugar (optional)		Fresh chestnut flour
		Sweetened whipped cream (optional)
		Fresh ricotta cheese (optional)

Fill a pot half full with spring water and bring it to a boil. When it's boiling, add a little salt, turn the heat to low, and add the chestnut flour a fistful at a time, sprinkling it into the water and stirring in the same direction constantly. Keep adding the flour and stirring until it reaches a thick consistency. The mixture will take 30 minutes to cook. Keep an additional kettle of boiling spring water on the side to add if the mixture becomes too dry.

When it is done, you should be able to pour it slowly—like a thick batter —onto a wooden board. Scoop it off the board and eat it hot with sweetened whipped cream or fresh ricotta.

COOKIES AND TARTS

The few desserts we eat in Tuscany are not very elaborate. The most famous ones were not invented to advance culinary art but originated in the home as a daily treat for the children—and maybe even their fathers.

We don't have much puff pastry, no mountains of cream or mousse. We like tarts that are always built around some kind of fruit or jam on a crunchy crust. We also like sponge cakes with pignolis, almonds, or walnuts and honey. Most desserts tend to be spongy and crunchy, not smooth and puffy.

The recipes that follow are the most popular of Tuscan desserts, which, of course, were originated by the peasants out of fantasy and the ingredients that were available.

The tarts seem to be larger and more elaborate versions of the regional cookies we start with. They are like cookies baked in a size large enough for a family.

There is no great work involved in baking these desserts, but, unlike the other recipes in this book that can only improve through personal creativity, these desserts require specific guidelines that never change. This is a characteristic peculiar to most desserts.

BISCOTTI DI PRATO

PRATO COOKIES

Prato is a little town near Florence, known for its textile industry and its cookies. The cookies are also called i cantucci di Prato *because they are cut diagonally.*

PANTRY	COLD STORAGE	MARKET
2½ cups sugar	4 eggs, separated	1 teaspoon vanilla extract
1 cup blanched, toasted, and chopped almonds		Peel of half an orange, grated
4 cups pastry flour		1 teaspoon baking powder
		½ cup toasted and chopped hazelnuts

Preheat oven to 400°F. Whip the egg whites in a bowl until firm. Add sugar, vanilla, orange peel, and egg yolks and mix well. Stir in baking powder and flour. Work into a dough, adding the nuts as you knead. It's hard work, as the dough should be very stiff.

Moisten your hands and divide the dough into pieces about the size of your fist. Shape each piece of dough into a strip about 1 inch thick and 2 inches wide. Flatten the dough slightly on the sides with the palm of your hand, leaving the dough somewhat domed in the center.

Dust a greased baking sheet with flour, put the strips on the sheet, leaving an inch or so between them, and place in the oven. As soon as the dough begins to color (about 10 or 15 minutes), take the strips out of the oven and turn oven down to 275°. Let the dough cool a bit—at least 10 minutes—then slice it crosswise into slices about 1 inch thick.

Put the cookies back in the oven and continue to bake. Start to check them in about 15 minutes to see if they have dried out—that's the way you want them, and that's why they are always dipped in good Vin Santo.

MAKES 4 TO 5 DOZEN COOKIES

I BRUTTI MA BUONI

THE UGLY BUT GOOD

*T*hese cookies are similar to Biscotti di Prato (preceding page), but they are made in Pistoia, Lucca, and even in the Piedmont, which is in a northern region of Italy. Nobody knows which cookie came first—this one or the Pratesi. But both are very good, so who cares? They don't come out looking beautiful, but they taste great.

PANTRY	COLD STORAGE	MARKET
2 cups sugar	6 egg whites	1 ½ cups chopped mixed almonds and hazelnuts, toasted
Flour	Unsalted butter	

Preheat oven to 275°F. Whip the egg whites in a bowl, adding the sugar gradually as you beat. When the egg whites are firm—not stiff, but resembling a shiny cake icing—add the nuts. Put the mixture in a double boiler and stir until it gets dense. (The mixture will quickly lose its volume and "melt.")

Grease a baking sheet and then dust it with flour. Drop the dough by spoonfuls, a couple of inches apart, onto the baking sheet and place in oven. The cookies should dry out rather than bake. Check the cookies in about 30 minutes—they are ready when they are dried out and have turned golden. This can take up to an hour. Let cookies cool completely before removing from cookie sheet.

VARIATION The flavor of these cookies can be changed by adding the grated peel of half a lemon or orange or a sprinkling of cinnamon to the egg-white mixture as you cook it in the double boiler.

MAKES APPROXIMATELY 7 DOZEN COOKIES

I CENCI

SWEET LITTLE RUGS

This is a typical dessert of the Tuscan countryside. My mother used it as a trap when my brothers and I were boys. After we came home from school, we always had a few hours to play before we had to come into the house to do our homework. We would try to pretend we didn't hear her, but she knew she could get us inside if she called, "Pino, Ricardo, Luca! I Cenci sono pronti per merenda!" (The Cenci are ready for your 5 o'clock snack!) Once we were inside, the door was locked behind us.

PANTRY	COLD STORAGE	MARKET
2 cups pastry flour	4 eggs, lightly beaten	3 tablespoons sweet vermouth
¼ cup granulated sugar	Grated peel of 1 lemon	½ tablespoon dry yeast, dissolved in a little warm milk
Salt	¼ cup (½ stick) butter, melted	
Olive oil		Confectioner's sugar

Put the flour on a flat surface and, in the center, make a crater deep enough to comfortably hold the eggs, granulated sugar, lemon peel, vermouth, a few pinches of salt, and melted butter. Fold the flour over into the middle of the crater and mix everything well with your hands.

When mixture is well blended and mushy, make a few holes in the center with your fingers and pour in the yeast mixture. Work the dough well until it is elastic enough to be rolled out. Pinch off a few generous pieces of dough and roll each as thin as possible, working one piece at a time until it is all rolled out.

With a pastry wheel in your hand, your fantasy is in charge. Cut the dough into any shapes you like—strips, circles, squares, bowties. Set them aside and repeat the process until all the dough is used up.

Place enough olive oil in a deep pan so the Cenci can float. Turn the heat on to medium and, when the oil is hot but not smoking, add the Cenci in batches, leaving room for them to remain separate. Turn them as they fry—which will be very quickly—and remove as soon as they are golden.

Drain them on paper towels and, when the excess oil is gone, sprinkle with confectioner's sugar. Cenci are good hot or at room temperature. You can keep them for a day or so, but if you leave them out they'll be gone before that. These cookies come in all shapes and sizes, and are crunchy but as light as air. My brothers and I could eat a whole batch in one sitting.

LA BUONISSIMA
WALNUT AND HONEY TART

PANTRY	COLD STORAGE	MARKET
Olive oil		½ cup honey, warmed
2 cups shelled walnuts		
Pasta Frolla (opposite page)		

Preheat oven to 350°F. Use the pastry dough to line a 9-inch pie pan. Moisten the walnuts with warm honey and place them in the shape of a dome to cover the bottom crust. Cover the walnut mixture with dough for the top crust, crimp edges, brush top with warm honey, and place in preheated oven. Start to check for doneness in about 15 minutes— the tart is ready when a golden brown dome forms on top. It should take about 30 minutes.

SCHIACCIATA CON L'UVA
GRAPE TART

PANTRY	COLD STORAGE	MARKET
Olive oil		Grapes, red seedless, washed and removed from stems
Sugar		
Pasta Frolla (opposite page)		

Preheat oven to 350°F. Roll out half of the dough and lay it in the bottom of an oiled, 1-inch-deep tart pan. Place a single layer of grapes on the crust and fill in any spaces with extra grapes.

Roll out the remaining dough and lay it on top of the tart. Brush a little olive oil on top of the crust and sprinkle with sugar. Place in the oven and bake for about half an hour. When the tart starts to smell sweet, check it to see if it's getting brown. When the crust looks crisp and light brown, it's done. Let cool to room temperature before serving.

PASTA FROLLA
PER TORTE E CROSTATE
DOUGH FOR PIES AND TARTS

PANTRY	COLD STORAGE	MARKET
2 cups pastry flour	1 cup (2 sticks) butter, softened	1 cup superfine sugar
	4 egg yolks and 1 white	

Make a crater in the flour and in the center add all the other ingredients. Mix well. Work the dough until it is the consistency of paste, but a bit firmer and very smooth. Don't worry if it sticks to the bottom of the table; just add a bit more flour as needed until not sticky. (This dough can be prepared a day in advance and refrigerated.) Divide the dough into 2 equal parts and roll out each half to a circle ⅛ inch thick —one for the bottom crust and one for the top.

LA ZUPPA INGLESE

ENGLISH CUSTARD

Zuppa Inglese is not English in origin, as many people think. It was invented by the peasant ladies in the Fiesole area who worked in the villas of the rich English people.

PANTRY	COLD STORAGE	MARKET
1 tablespoon flour	4 egg yolks	1 pound *savoiardi* (see Note)
4 tablespoons sugar	4 cups milk	
4 tablespoons confectioner's sugar	Grated peel from one lemon	
½ cup Vin Santo		

Put egg yolks in a pot, whip them slightly, mix in the flour, and put over very low heat on the stove. Immediately stir in the milk and, continuing to stir constantly in one direction, add—one at a time—the sugar, lemon peel, confectioner's sugar, and Vin Santo. Continue to stir as the mixture heats through. Do not let it boil, but let it cook until it thickens just slightly, so that it will coat a wooden spoon with a thin film. Stir in the whole *savoiardi*. (Try to keep the *savoiardi* from breaking as you stir, but if they do break, don't worry about it.) Take mixture off the heat right away—it will have the consistency of thick cream and will thicken as it cools in the refrigerator. Pour the mixture in a bowl and let it refrigerate for an hour. That's it.

NOTE Italian ladyfingers—*savoiardi*—are available in many Italian bakeries and are larger and drier than the American version. If *savoiardi* are not available, you can use American ladyfingers.

SERVES 4

TIRAMISÙ

Tiramisù *means "pick-me-up" because of its energetic combination of egg yolks, sugar, rum, and espresso. In Italy we still dispute its origins, but we won't do that here because even if it's not Tuscan, it's so good we don't care where it comes from.*

PANTRY	COLD STORAGE	MARKET
1 ½ tablespoons sugar	3 egg yolks	4 teaspoons dark rum
		½ pound mascarpone cheese
		1 ½ cups strong espresso, cooled
		24 (about 1 pound) *savoiardi* (Italian ladyfingers), toasted (see Note)
		Semisweet chocolate shavings

Beat the yolks and the sugar until very light. Beat in 2 teaspoons of the rum and then beat in the mascarpone until the mixture is smooth. Beat in 2 teaspoons of the espresso until everything is well mixed.

Add the remaining rum to the remaining espresso and quickly dip each ladyfinger into it—but don't soak them or they will fall apart. Make a layer of ladyfingers in the bottom of a baking dish.

Spoon the mascarpone mixture over the ladyfingers, cover with plastic wrap, and refrigerate for at least 30 minutes. Sprinkle top with chocolate and cut into squares before serving.

NOTE Toast the ladyfingers in a 375°F. oven for 15 minutes to dry them.

SERVES 4

P. S.
LAST NIGHT
IN FLORENCE

I used to live in a house in Florence on top of a roof—a very small house, but right in the middle of the sky. My apartment had a tiny bedroom with a terrace that was about fifty-five times the size of the whole apartment. It was the terrace for everyone in the building, but no one came up to my floor because it was too many flights up and there was no elevator. I had to think twice before I left home.

It was with a mixture of excitement and sadness that I left Tuscany in 1980. I left with the idea that I would come back in about six months, but I was very sad because I knew I was going to abandon my best friends—the kind of friends you fool around with and whom you are very serious and honest with, whom you know in a way that you can know only a few people in your life.

We were all involved in one way or another in the theater. One of us was a stage director, one was a writer, and three or four of us were actors. Because I hate saying good-bye and I wanted to avoid any parties, I told them I was leaving two days later than I actually was, but somehow they managed to find out anyway.

They surprised me while I was at home packing—Claudio the Nut, Marcos the Fat, Gianni the "Chicchero," all of them. It was one of those beautiful October evenings, still light, and I was running around the terrace in my bathing suit, trying to decide what to do with all the plants and flowers and tomatoes I had been growing in huge terra-cotta pots. When I saw those guys appear, with their tongues down to their knees from the climb, I knew they were coming because I was leaving Florence. They brought plenty of food, bread, and wine to celebrate with. Actors, writers, stage directors—all of us big eaters.

Slowly, after the first glass of wine and the second glass of wine, and after the fifteen minutes of fooling around, we started to set up a dinner. First we had a very simple and quickly made appetizer with fava beans and pecorino cheese. In Tuscany we usually don't serve fava beans out of the shell; we just put them out on the table with the pecorino, and each person helps himself to some beans, takes them out of the shell, and, with a piece of bread and a piece of the cheese, eats everything at the same time.

There were still four or five tomatoes left on my tomato plant, so we made a pasta dish with fresh tomatoes, olive oil, and garlic. I don't think I even had any basil in the house, but the tomatoes were so good and ripe, we just sliced them into the hot olive oil and garlic; then, when the spaghetti was done, we let the tomatoes warm inside the pan. It was perfect.

But the greatest thing were the anchovies that Gianni the Chicchero brought. He was "Chicchero" because he would say "chi-chi-chi" all the time, even when he was eating. When he kissed you, he missed your cheek and got one eye because he had a nervous tic. The one we knew best was when he would look through the hole made with his thumb and finger and say "pop-pop-pop." He always did this to show appreciation and happiness when he was with his friends and there was a huge bottle of wine on the table. His life was complete. Friends, fun, and wine—no problem. What more do you want?

Anchovies were Gianni's favorite dish, and he knew I would make them the way my mother used to, and the way he loved to eat them—just slightly poached in wine, olive oil, and garlic. We put these anchovies in the middle of the table and Chicchero, who is basically a clown, would dip two slices of bread into the plate of anchovies, squeeze some anchovies between the bread, and put the whole thing in his mouth. He would suck the juice from the bread and eat it with the anchovies. He was an incredible character.

This dinner went on and on for hours and hours. When everyone left it was eight in the morning and we had drunk every drop of wine and eaten every last crumb in the house. That was my farewell to Tuscany.

INDEX

Anchovy(-ies)
  Dante's sweet mess, 51
  dressing, puntarelle salad
    with, 213
  gratinéed, 148
  in olive oil, 147
appetizers, 42–55
  artichoke frittata, 49
  bean salad, 54
  chicken liver pâté,
    Florentine style, 47
  Dante's sweet mess, 51
  eggplant frittata, 50
  eggs with truffles, 48
  fettunta, 43
  fettunta with clams, 44–45
  fettunta with tomatoes, 44
  game liver crostini, 46
  Giancarlo's garlic bread with
    porcini, 48
  marinated eel, 132
  prosciutto and figs, 52
  raw fava beans with sheep's
    milk cheese, 55
  toasted bread with chopped
    tomato, 45
apples, baked, 223
arborio rice, 34
artichoke(s)
  and carrots, salad of,
    214–215
  fried baby, 208
  frittata, 49
  and lamb stew, 194

Basil, 31, 33
bass sauce, spaghetti with, 113
bay leaves, 31–32, 33
bean(s), 35, 53
  and pasta soup, 83
  raw fava, with sheep's milk
    cheese, 55
  salad, 54
beef
  beefsteak, Florentine
    style, 190
  mixed boiled meats, 182
  pot roast, Florentine style,
    184–185
  sliced steak, Florentine
    style, 191

bowtie pasta, *see* farfalle
bread, 34–35
  chicken liver pâté,
    Florentine style, 47
  and fish stew, 151
  game liver crostini, 46
  salad, 215
  with tomatoes, 44
bread, toasted garlic, 31, 43
  with chopped tomato, 45
  with clams, 44–45
  with porcini, Giancarlo's, 48
bread soup, 71–79
  cauliflower and, 75
  gardener's, 73
  onion, Maremma style, 72
  "overcooked" vegetable
    and, 78
  tomato and, 79
  woodsman's, 74
bresaola, stuffed morels with,
    62–63
broccoli rabe
  sautéed, 208
  spaghetti with radicchio
    and, 112
brutti ma buoni, 228
buonissima, 230

Cacciucco, 151
calf's liver with sage, 181
capers
  Dante's sweet mess, 51
  sole with, 142
capon, roasted stuffed, 203
carrots, salad of artichokes
    and, 214–215
catmint, 31
cauliflower and bread soup, 75
cenci, 229
cheese
  goat, spaghettini with
    pepper and, 110–111
  mozzarella, farfalle with
    tomatoes, basil and, 101
  Parmesan, rotelle with
    tomato sauce and, 116
  ricotta, rotelle with
    cinnamon and, 115
  sheep's milk, raw fava beans
    with, 55
chestnuts, roasted, 224–225
chicken
  devil-style free-range, 200
  hunter's style, 199

  with lemon, 199
  liver pâté, Florentine
    style, 47
  livers sautéed in black butter
    and sage, 182
  mixed boiled meats, 182
  roasted stuffed capon, 203
  stuffed breasts of, with
    mushroom sauce, 201
chick-pea
  bean salad, 54
  soup, 81
chocolate, baked peaches
    stuffed with walnuts and,
    224
clams
  cold seafood salad, Tuscan
    style, 136
  fettunta with, 44–45
  risotto, fisherman's
    style, 126
  spaghetti, pirate style, 106
  steamed with garlic and
    white wine, 144
clam sauce, white
  risotto in, 125
  spaghetti in, 110
cookies
  brutti ma buoni, 228
  cenci, 229
  Prato, 227
cornmeal mush, *see* polenta
crab, soft-shell, soup, 144–145
cremini mushrooms
  grilled, 59
  salad of, 60
crostini
  Florentine style, 47
  game liver, 46
  with porcini, Giancarlo's, 48
custard, English, 232
cuttlefish
  black, stew, 156
  black rice stewed with, 127

Dante's sweet mess, 51
desserts, 217–233
  baked peaches stuffed
    with walnuts and
    chocolate, 224
  baked pears or apples, 223
  brutti ma buoni, 228
  buonissima, 230
  cenci, 229

dough for pies and
   tarts, 230
dried figs and walnuts, 221
English custard, 232
fruit salad, 222
grape tart, 231
orange salad, 222–223
peaches in red wine, 221
Prato cookies, 227
roasted chestnuts, 224–225
strawberries in vinegar, 220
sweet polenta, 225
tiramisù, 233
walnut and honey tart, 230
dough for pies and tarts, 230
dressing, salad, 211
duck
   with dry vermouth, 163
   with orange sauce, 164

Easter lamb, 193
eggplant
   frittata, 50
   spaghetti, Maremma
     style, 109
   in stuffed mushroom
     caps, 63
eggs
   artichoke frittata, 49
   eggplant frittata, 50
   Italian omelette with
     pasta, 117
   with truffles, 48
English custard, 232

Farfalle
   with sun-dried
     tomatoes, 102
   with tomatoes, mozzarella,
     and basil, 101
fava beans, raw, with sheep's
   milk cheese, 55
fettunta, 31, 43
   with clams, 44–45
   with tomatoes, 44
figs
   dried, and walnuts, 221
   prosciutto and, 52
fish, 129–159
   anchovies in olive oil, 147
   baby octopus stew, 155
   and bread stew, Tuscan
     style, 151
   choosing of, 134
   cleaning of, 134

cold, and vegetable
   salad, 135
cold seafood salad, Tuscan
   style, 136
devil-style mullet, 143
fried sardines, 148
gratinéed anchovies, 148
grilled octopus, 154
grilled tuna with a marinade
   of pesto and vinaigrette,
   140–141
marinated eel, 132
roasted sole, 136
roasted with potatoes, 137
sardines in white wine, 149
sole with capers, 142
spaghetti with sea bass
   sauce, 113
trout or baby salmon with
   balsamic vinegar, 139
tuna steak, Livornese
   style, 140
whole baby grouper or red
   snapper poached in
   tomato sauce, 138
see also shellfish; squid
frittata
   artichoke, 49
   eggplant, 50
fruit salad, 222

Game, 161–175
   duck with dry
     vermouth, 163
   duck with orange sauce, 164
   liver crostini, 46
   marinade for squab and
     rabbit, 170
   pheasant, hunter's style, 165
   quail and sausage with
     polenta, 167
   roasted quail with
     tarragon, 166
   sauce, tagliatelle with,
     96–97
   squab, Salmi style, 169
   squab stew with
     mushrooms, 168
   venison marinade, 175
   venison with Marsala wine,
     174–175
   see also rabbit
gardener's soup, 73
garlic bread, toasted, 31, 43
   with chopped tomato, 45

with clams, 44–45
with porcini, Giancarlo's, 48
Giancarlo's garlic bread with
   porcini, 48
goat cheese, spaghettini with
   pepper and, 110–111
grape tart, 231
green sauce, piquant, 183
grouper, whole baby, poached
   in tomato sauce, 138

Herbs, 31–33
honey and walnut tart, 230

Ingredients, 28–35
Italian omelette with
   pasta, 117

Kidneys, grilled pork, 189

Lamb
   and artichoke stew, 194
   Easter, 193
   sauce, tagliatelle with, 92
   and sweet pepper stew, 195
lentil(s)
   bean salad, 54
   pork sausage and, 187
   soup, 82
liver
   calf's, with sage, 181
   chicken, pâté, Florentine
     style, 47
   chicken, sautéed in black
     butter and sage, 182
   game, crostini, 46

Macedonia, 222
marinades
   for squab and rabbit, 170
   venison, 175
Marsala wine, venison with,
   174–175
meats, 177–195
   mixed boiled, 182
   oxtail stew, 180–181
   sweetbreads sautéed in black
     butter and sage, 182
   tagliatelle with game sauce,
     96–97
   venison marinade, 175
   venison with Marsala wine,
     174–175
   see also beef; lamb; pork;
     rabbit; veal

mint, 31, 32, 33
morels stuffed with bresaola, 62–63
mozzarella, farfalle with tomatoes, basil, and, 101
mullet, devil-style, 143
mushroom(s), 58–67
  caps, stuffed, 63
  eggs with truffles, 48
  fresh, risotto with, 121
  Giancarlo's garlic bread with porcini, 48
  grilled cremini, 59
  grilled porcini, 67
  mixed wild, with prosciutto, 62
  penne with red porcini sauce, 104
  porcini, 64–66
  salad of cremini, 60
  sautéed, with balsamic vinegar, 60–61
  soup, 84
  spaghetti, Maremma style, 109
  squab stew with, 168
  stuffed morels with bresaola, 62–63
  tagliatelle in white porcini sauce, 95
  tagliatelle with porcini and butter, 97
  tagliolini with white or black truffles, 93
  wild, sautéed a different way, 61
mushroom sauce, 98–99
  penne baked with sausage and, 100–101
  red, penne with, 98
  stuffed breasts of chicken with, 201
  white, penne in, 99
mussels
  risotto, fisherman's style, 126
  spaghetti, pirate style, 106

Nepitella, 31

Octopus
  baby, stew, 155
  grilled, 154–155
odori, 30–31

olive oil, 30
olives, black, rabbit stew with, 173
omelette with pasta, Italian, 117
onion soup, Maremma style, 72
orange(s)
  radicchio garnished and scented with, 214
  salad, 222–223
  sauce, duck with, 164
oregano, 32, 33
ossobuco in wine and tarragon sauce, 185
"overcooked" bread and vegetable soup, 78
oxtail stew, 180–181

Parmesan cheese, rotelle with tomato sauce and, 116
parsley, 32
pasta, 34, 90–117
  farfalle with sun-dried tomatoes, 102
  farfalle with tomatoes, mozzarella, and basil, 101
  Italian omelette with, 117
  peasant-style rigatoni, 107
  rotelle with ricotta and cinnamon, 115
  rotelle with tomato sauce and Parmesan cheese, 116
  tagliolini with white or black truffles, 93
  see also penne; spaghetti; tagliatelle
pasta soups
  bean and, 83
  chick-pea, 81
  lentil, 82
pâté, chicken liver, Florentine style, 47
peaches
  baked, stuffed with walnuts and chocolate, 224
  in red wine, 221
pears, baked, 223
peas
  peasant-style risotto, 123
  risotto with, 122–123
  squid, fisherman's style, 152

penne
  baked with mushroom sauce and sausage, 100–101
  with red mushroom sauce, 98
  with red porcini sauce, 104
  with ricotta and cinnamon, 115
  with rude sauce, 103
  with sage and veal, 100
  in white mushroom sauce, 99
pepper, hot red, 35
  spaghetti with garlic, olive oil and, 111
pepper, sweet
  Dante's sweet mess, 51
  stew, lamb and, 195
pesto sauce, 141
  and vinaigrette, grilled tuna with a marinade of, 140–141
pheasant, hunter's style, 165
pies, dough for, 230
pignolis, 35
pinwheel pasta, see rotelle
piquant green sauce, 183
polenta, 87
  black cuttlefish stew with, 156
  quail and sausage with, 167
  sweet, 225
porcini mushrooms, 64–66
  Giancarlo's garlic bread with, 48
  grilled, 67
  sauce, penne with, 104
  sauce, tagliatelle in, 95
  tagliatelle with butter and, 97
pork
  grilled spareribs, 189
  kidneys, grilled, 189
  sausage and lentils, 187
potatoes
  fish roasted with, 137
  roast rabbit with, 174
  stuffed morels with bresaola, 62–63
pot roast, Florentine style, 184–185
poultry, 197–203
  duck with dry vermouth, 163
  duck with orange sauce, 164

game liver crostini, 46
marinade for squab and
    rabbit, 170
mixed boiled meats, 182
pheasant, hunter's style, 165
quail and sausage with
    polenta, 167
roasted quail with
    tarragon, 166
squab, Salmi style, 169
squab stew with
    mushrooms, 168
tagliatelle with game sauce,
    96–97
see also chicken
Prato cookies, 227
prosciutto
    and figs, 52
    mixed wild mushrooms
        with, 62
puntarelle salad with anchovy
    dressing, 213

Quail
    roasted, with tarragon, 166
    and sausage with
        polenta, 167
quill-shaped pasta, *see* penne

Rabbit
    fricassée, 171
    hunter's style, 172
    roast, with potatoes, 174
    and squab, marinade
        for, 170
    stew with black olives, 173
radicchio
    garnished and scented with
        oranges, 214
    spaghetti with broccoli rabe
        and, 112
ribollita, 78
rice
    arborio, 34
    black, stewed with
        cuttlefish, 127
    see also risotto
ricotta, rotelle with cinnamon
    and, 115
rigatoni, peasant-style, 107
risotto, 119–127
    black, stewed with cuttlefish,
        or black squid, 127
    fisherman's style, 126
    with fresh mushrooms, 121

with green peas, 122–123
peasant-style, 123
with spinach, 122
with tomatoes and basil, 124
in white clam sauce, 125
roast, Florentine style,
    184–185
rosemary, 31, 32, 33
rotelle
    with ricotta and
        cinnamon, 115
    with tomato sauce and
        Parmesan cheese, 116

Sage, 31, 32, 33
salad(s), 210–215
    of artichokes and carrots,
        214–215
    bean, 54
    bread, 215
    cold fish and vegetable, 135
    cold seafood, Tuscan
        style, 136
    of cremini mushrooms, 60
    dressing, 211
    fruit, 222
    orange, 222–223
    puntarelle, with anchovy
        dressing, 213
    radicchio garnished
        and scented with
        oranges, 214
salmon, Coho, with balsamic
    vinegar, 139
sardines
    fried, 148
    in white wine, 149
sauces
    mushroom, 98–99
    pesto, 141
    piquant green, 183
sausage
    mixed wild mushrooms with
        prosciutto, 62
    penne baked with
        mushroom sauce and,
        100–101
    pork, and lentils, 187
    prosciutto and figs, 52
    and quail with polenta, 167
scampi, breaded and
    broiled, 159
seafood salad, cold, Tuscan
    style, 136

sheep's milk cheese, raw fava
    beans with, 55
shellfish
    black cuttlefish stew, 156
    breaded and broiled
        shrimp, 159
    clams steamed with garlic
        and white wine, 144
    cold seafood salad, Tuscan
        style, 136
    fettunta with clams, 44–45
    fish and bread stew, Tuscan
        style, 151
    grilled shrimp, 158
    risotto, fisherman's
        style, 126
    risotto in white clam
        sauce, 125
    shrimp, fisherman's
        style, 159
    snail stew, 157
    soft-shell crab soup,
        144–145
    spaghetti, pirate style, 106
    spaghetti in white clam
        sauce, 110
shrimp
    breaded and broiled, 159
    cold seafood salad, Tuscan
        style, 136
    fisherman's style, 159
    grilled, 158
    risotto, fisherman's
        style, 126
    spaghetti, pirate style, 106
snail stew, 157
snapper, red, poached in
    tomato sauce, 138
sole
    with capers, 142
    roasted, 136
soups, 70–84
    bread, 71–79
    cauliflower and bread, 75
    chick-pea, 81
    gardener's, 73
    lentil, 82
    mushroom, 84
    onion, Maremma style, 72
    "overcooked" bread and
        vegetable, 78
    pasta and bean, 83
    soft-shell crab, 144–145
    tomato and bread, 79
    woodsman's, 74

spaghetti
with broccoli rabe and
radicchio, 112
with fresh tomato sauce, 105
with garlic, olive oil, and hot
pepper, 111
Maremma style, 109
pirate style, 106
rustic-style, 104–105
with sea bass sauce, 113
spaghettini with goat cheese
and pepper, 110–111
in white clam sauce, 110
spareribs, grilled, 189
spinach
risotto with, 122
squid and, 154
stuffed squid, Florentine
style, 153
squab
and rabbit, marinade
for, 170
Salmi style, 169
stew with mushrooms, 168
squid
black, black rice stewed
with, 127
cold seafood salad, Tuscan
style, 136
fisherman's style, 152
risotto, fisherman's
style, 126
spaghetti, pirate style, 106
and spinach, 154
stuffed, Florentine style, 153
steak, sliced, Florentine
style, 191
stews
artichoke and lamb, 194
baby octopus, 155
black cuttlefish, 156
fish and bread, 151
lamb and sweet pepper, 195
oxtail, 180–181
rabbit, with black olives, 173
snail, 157
squab, with
mushrooms, 168
stocking a Tuscan kitchen,
28–35

strawberries in vinegar, 220
sweetbreads sautéed in black
butter and sage, 182
sweet little rugs, 229
sweet polenta, 225

Tagliatelle
with flavors of the kitchen
garden, 94–95
with game sauce, 96–97
with lamb sauce, 92
with porcini and butter, 97
in white porcini sauce, 95
tagliolini with white or black
truffles, 93
tarragon, 31, 32
tarts
dough for, 230
grape, 231
walnut and honey, 230
thyme, 31, 32, 33
tiramisù, 233
tomato(es), 33–34
and bread soup, 79
bread with, 44
chopped, toasted bread
with, 45
farfalle with mozzarella,
basil and, 101
fettunta with clams and, 45
risotto with basil and, 124
sun-dried, farfalle with, 102
tomato sauce
fresh, spaghetti with, 105
rotelle with Parmesan cheese
and, 116
whole baby grouper or red
snapper poached in, 138
tongue, in mixed boiled meats,
182
truffles
eggs with, 48
white or black, tagliolini
with, 93
tuna
grilled, with a marinade of
pesto and vinaigrette,
140–141
steak, Livornese style, 140

Ugly but good cookies, 228

Veal
liver with sage, 181
penne with sage and, 100
shank in wine and tarragon
sauce, 185
vegetable(s)
and bread soup,
"overcooked," 78
and cold fish salad, 135
grilled, 209
tagliatelle with flavors of the
kitchen garden, 94–95
see also salads; specific
vegetables
venison
marinade, 175
with Marsala wine, 174–175
vinaigrette and pesto, grilled
tuna with a marinade of,
140–141
vinegar, 35
strawberries in, 220
vinegar, balsamic, 35
sautéed mushrooms with,
60–61
trout or baby salmon
with, 139

Walnut(s)
baked peaches stuffed with
chocolate and, 224
dried figs and, 221
and honey tart, 230
wine
Marsala, venison with,
174–175
red, peaches in, 221
red, and tarragon sauce, veal
shank in, 185
white, clams steamed with
garlic and, 144
white, sardines in, 149
woodsman's soup, 74

Zucchini, in gardener's
soup, 73